JUSTIN TIMBERLAKE

A Biography

Kimberly Dillon Summers

GREENWOOD BIOGRAPHIES

 GREENWOOD

AN IMPRINT OF ABC-CLIO, LLC
Santa Barbara, California • Denver, Colorado • Oxford, England

Library of Congress Cataloging-in-Publication Data

Summers, Kimberly Dillon.
   Justin Timberlake : a biography / Kimberly Dillon Summers.
      p. cm. — (Greenwood biographies)
   Includes bibliographical references and index.
   ISBN 978-0-313-38320-5 (print : alk. paper) — ISBN 978-0-313-38321-2 (ebook)   1. Timberlake, Justin, 1981–   2. Singers—United States—Biography. I. Title.
   ML420.T537S86   2010
   782.42164092—dc22
   [B]   2010015230

ISBN: 978-0-313-38320-5
EISBN: 978-0-313-38321-2

14 13 12 11 10   1 2 3 4 5

This book is also available on the World Wide Web as an eBook.
Visit www.abc-clio.com for details.

Greenwood
An Imprint of ABC-CLIO, LLC

ABC-CLIO, LLC
130 Cremona Drive, P.O. Box 1911
Santa Barbara, California 93116-1911

This book is printed on acid-free paper ∞

Manufactured in the United States of America

JUSTIN TIMBERLAKE

Recent Titles in Greenwood Biographies

CONTENTS

CONTENTS

SERIES FOREWORD

In response to high school and public library needs, Greenwood developed this distinguished series of full-length biographies specifically for student use. Prepared by field experts and professionals, these engaging biographies are tailored for high school students who need challenging yet accessible biographies. Ideal for secondary school assignments, the length, format, and subject areas are designed to meet educators' requirements and students' interests.

Greenwood offers an extensive selection of biographies spanning all curriculum-related subject areas including social studies, the sciences, literature and the arts, history and politics, as well as popular culture, covering public figures and famous personalities from all time periods and backgrounds, both historical and contemporary, who have made an impact on American and/or world culture. Greenwood biographies were chosen based on comprehensive feedback from librarians and educators. Consideration was given to both curriculum relevance and inherent interest. The result is an intriguing mix of the well known and unexpected, that saints and sinners from long-ago history and contemporary pop culture. Readers will find a wide array of subject choices from fascinating crime figures like Al Capone to inspiring pioneers like Margaret Mead, from the greatest minds of our time like Stephen Hawking to the most amazing success stories of our day like J. K. Rowling.

Although the emphasis is on fact, not glorification, the books are meant to be fun to read. Each volume provides in-depth information about the subject's life from birth to childhood, the teen years, and adulthood. A thorough account relates family background and education, traces personal and professional influences, and explores struggles, accomplishments, and contributions. A timeline highlights the most significant life events against a historical perspective. Bibliographies supplement the reference value of each volume.

OVERVIEW

Justin Timberlake has been a very important asset to the music business. He has proven his musical talent by first playing in a boy band and then stemming off into a successful solo career. He has also expanded his resume to include actor, business owner, and fund-raiser. Justin knows his celebrity comes with risk and sometimes a lack of privacy.

Justin Randall Timberlake was born January 31, 1981, in Memphis, Tennessee, to Lynn Bomar and Randall Timberlake. Education was a very important aspect of Justin's life. Even during his stint on *The All-New Mickey Mouse Club,* he had tutors on the set. His family, especially his parents and his grandparents, have supported him through every aspect of his career. Justin had performed in many talent shows at school, and, at age 11, he performed on *Star Search.* This would be the beginning of a long and lucrative career.

When Justin became one of the Mouseketeers on *The All-New Mickey Mouse Club,* he had no idea the contacts he was making. He starred with future superstars Britney Spears and Christina Aguilera, and JC Chasez and Nikki *DeLoach.* This was where Justin learned about performing before live audiences and keeping their attention. He did musical numbers and comedic skits, which would help him later as the host of *Saturday Night Live*. Most importantly, this opportunity gave Justin the drive and determination to be a successful singer. For Justin, it was the clincher to what he wanted to do for the rest of his life. After *The All-New Mickey Mouse Club* was cancelled, Justin returned home to Tennessee and to his elementary school. Despite the success Justin had on the show, he was more than comfortable returning to school, and those who knew him back home treated him no differently, despite his budding stardom.

With his connections from *The All-New Mickey Mouse Club*, the group 'NSync was formed. Chasez, with producer Lou Pearlman, convinced Justin to return to Orlando, Florida, and form the band. Justin's mother, Lynn, is said to have put together 'NSync's name with the last letters of each band member's first name (after Jason Galasso left the band and Lance Bass replaced him, the formula still worked as Lance's full name is Langston). She was also the group's den mother in the Orlando home the band shared. With Lance Bass, Chris Kirkpatrick, JC Chasez, and Joey Fatone, the boy band released their first album, titled *NSYNC, in September 2006. The album was released first in Germany and then in the United States. To promote their album, the band toured across the nation. Similar to the Backstreet Boys and Boys II Men, 'NSync was captivating thanks to their boyish good looks and their music. 'NSync went on to record *Home for Christmas, No Strings Attached*, and *Celebrity*. Before the release of *No Strings Attached*, the band had a contract dispute with producer Pearlman and RCA Records. After a lawsuit, the two sides settled out of court. The albums *No Strings Attached* and *Celebrity* were released with Jive Records. With the band's success came a new line of merchandising including hats, T-shirts, and dolls. To enhance matters, Justin's personal life became very public with his relationship with Britney Spears. Because of all the attention he was receiving in magazines and tabloids, Justin emerged and was seen as the lead person of 'NSync. After seven years of touring, recording, and writing, the 'NSync members went their separate ways. While Kirkpatrick and Fatone went into acting, Chasez began a solo music career just as Justin broke away to do the same. Bass wanted to be the first rock star in space, but also did some acting after 'NSync separated.

Justin's solo music career was fueled by his need to make a name for himself and by his breakup with Spears that received much public attention. His song "Cry Me a River" was said to have been written about his relationship with Spears. The video caused some controversy because of its implication of infidelity during the couple's relationship. Justin's first solo album, titled *Justified*, was released in November 2002. It was to evoke who Justin really was as a person and as a musician. The album won many awards for pop music and for the many collaborations with various musicians. As with other albums, Justin promoted it with a tour and included big names such as Christina Aguilera. In 2006, Justin produced his second solo album, *FutureSex/LoveSounds*. The album was successful with more than 2 million copies sold in the world. "Sexy Back," the first single released from the album, was played more than 80,000 times on MySpace alone. He has presented at many awards shows, including the *Grammy Awards*, *Teen Nick Awards*, and the *MTV Video Music Awards*. At many of these shows, aside from being a presenter, he also performed. Between recording his two solo albums, Justin made a living collaborating with several other artists including, Brian McKnight, Nelly, and will.i.am, among others.

In 2004, the famous wardrobe malfunction with Janet Jackson happened during the half-time show at the Super Bowl. What was supposed to happen was Justin was to undress Jackson down to a red garment underneath her shirt. What did happen was that Justin exposed Jackson's breast to millions of people watching the Super Bowl. Justin was credited with coining the phrase *wardrobe malfunction* after he used it in his apology. The pair was told to apologize publicly, or they would not be allowed to perform at the *Grammy Awards*. Justin did make a public apology before the *Grammy Awards* and also proceeded to apologize during the award presentation.

Despite all the negative publicity with the Super Bowl fiasco, Justin decided to try something new and different in the form of acting. His first film was *Edison Force*, which was released directly to video. It was his next film, *Alpha Dog*, which helped Justin make a name for himself in the film industry. Based on a true story, Justin played one of the gangsters in the film. He was nominated for many awards for his portrayal of Frankie Ballenbacher. His other film credits include *Southland Tales*, *Black Snake Moan*, and *The Love Guru*. He had voice-over parts in *Yogi Bear* and *Shrek the Third*. In 2009 and scheduled to continue in 2010, he is featured in *The Open Road* and *The Social Network*. Justin hasn't limited himself to just acting in films. He was also a host on *Saturday Night Live* and became well-known for his comedy skits with Andy Samberg. For his work on *Saturday Night Live*, he received many nominations and awards. He has appeared in many television commercials for Sony, Givenchy, and Pepsi.

Aside from his acting and music career, Justin has found his business sense as well. Together with his best friend, Trace Ayala, he created a clothing line, named William Rast. He is also a partner in a couple of restaurants on both coasts. Justin owns a line of tequila, called 901, named after the area code of Tennessee. As the owner of Tennman Records, Justin looks to find fresh musical talent. He also owns an eco-friendly golf course in his home state of Tennessee. His favorite sports include golf and basketball. He enjoys playing golf for leisure as it takes him away from the busyness of life for four or five hours.

Like many other celebrities, Justin's personal life has always remained a mystery as Justin tries to keep his private life out of the media spotlight. This has not always worked to his advantage, especially with his relationship with fellow Mouseketeer Britney Spears. After having an extensive relationship with the star, his breakup was front-page news. It did, however, give Justin new material for his first solo album. His love interests have included Cameron Diaz, Alyssa Milano, Scarlett Johansson, and Jessica Biel. Each time, stories have come up about the young celebrity getting married or breaking up with his love interest. In an interview with Oprah, he made sure not to say whom he was dating, just that he did have a girlfriend at the time.

Despite his busy schedule with music and acting, Justin also takes time to give back to his hometown and various charities. He signed a five-year contract to host the annual golf tournament for the Shriners' Hospital in Las Vegas. He has donated money to his elementary school, the Memphis Music Foundation, and the Memphis Rock and Roll Museum. He performed with the Rolling Stones at the SARS event in Toronto and sang with James Brown to raise money for the Asian tsunami. He donated money to the victims of Hurricane Katrina. He has used his love for golf to help charities and play in the Bob Hope Classic.

Throughout his life, he has always had the support of his family. His mother and stepfather continue to manage Justin's career, and he constantly cites his mother as a great influence on his life and career. He has never forgotten his hometown of Memphis where he first displayed his talents at a talent show at the local elementary school. Most of what makes Justin a celebrity is his ability to recognize everything in his life that has helped him be successful.

ACKNOWLEDGMENTS

Many thanks to all those who patiently and enthusiastically supported me through my publication. To my mother, Carol, and Steve, whose confidence and enthusiasm in my abilities has never waned; my brother, Bill, who helped me editorially; my sister, Tracy, my cheerleader; my children Lauren, Andrew, and Alex; and most of all, my best friend, critic, and husband, John. Thanks to all the editors at ABC-CLIO and my literary agent who have helped me every step of the way.

INTRODUCTION

Justin Timberlake began his singing career in a church choir and then graduated at the age of 11 to doing *Star Search*. Being chosen out of 20,000 contestants sent his career and confidence soaring. From that point, Justin's career has always moved forward to bigger and better things. Despite the fact that he lost on *Star Search*, he was confident in auditioning for *The All-New Mickey Mouse Club*, a role Justin had for two seasons until the show was cancelled for good in 1995. Since then, he has enjoyed success as a lead singer for a boy band, a musician, an actor, an entrepreneur, and a philanthropist.

His lead-singer career with the band 'NSync brought him to fame quickly. Justin had produced many albums and had written many songs. Teenagers were enamored with the pop music of this band but also with the attractiveness of its four members. After the breakup of the band, he had the ambition to make many more albums and continue to write songs on his own. Justin went on to have a solo career and made many appearances on award shows, on prime-time television, and at charity events. He has six Grammy Awards to his credit as well as many international and national awards. This determination to make himself known not only as a musician, but also as a celebrity makes people take notice of Justin. Those celebrities who enjoy the most success are versatile and have shown interest and success in areas other than acting and singing.

At the mere age of 29, Justin has sold billions of albums, acted in several films and TV movies, and started successful businesses. To teenagers, his quick rise to fame is one of inspiration and hope that you can do anything to which you set your mind. His family has inspired him since the very early days of his career as a Mouseketeer. His mother and stepfather manage Justin's career and are never far away from their prodigy. Justin's father also contributed to Justin's career by bringing music into the home via church choir and playing the guitar.

Justin has opened restaurants on both coasts. He has started a clothing line with one of his partners and most recently started his own music business. His philanthropy includes giving to charities such as the Memphis Music Foundation and to the Memphis Rock 'n' Soul Museum. A charity, established by Justin, gives to music education programs in elementary schools and emphasizes the positive effects music has on children. He has incorporated his love of basketball and golf in his charity work as well, using both as outlets to raise money for worthwhile causes.

Although his life as a musician and actor has flourished, like many celebrities, Justin has been surrounded by some scandal as well. His relationships with women have been a constant issue in magazines, especially with fellow *Mickey Mouse Club* star Britney Spears. At Super Bowl XXXVIII, he and Janet Jackson performed during the half-time show. During the half-time show, Justin removed a piece of Janet's clothing, accidentally exposing her breast momentarily and starting a frenzy throughout the nation about what people were viewing on television. As a punishment the two were obligated to apologize on national television in order to be able to attend the *Grammy Awards* a few weeks later.

Justin has done his best to stay out of the tabloids and has had a successful career. He continues to work as a musician and put his acting career on hold to pursue what he does best—singing and writing music. Justin's early career has shaped him into a determined adult. Because of his attractiveness and willingness to strive despite setbacks, fans are drawn to Justin Timberlake as both a person and a celebrity.

TIMELINE: EVENTS IN THE LIFE OF JUSTIN TIMBERLAKE

January 31, 1981	Justin Timberlake is born in Memphis, Tennessee, at St. Jude Hospital.
August 8, 1992	Justin competes in and wins Universal Charm Pageant, winning Best Model, Best Dressed, Best Sportswear, Most Handsome, and Supreme Winner.
1992	Justin competes on *Star Search*.
September 12, 1993	Brother Jonathan Perry is born to Randy and Lisa Timberlake.
1993	Justin joins *The All-New Mickey Mouse Club* for sixth and seventh seasons.
1995	Justin joins 'NSync.
October 22, 1995	'NSync has first public performance at Pleasure Island at Walt Disney World in Orlando, Florida.
October 1996	'NSync releases its first single, "I Want You Back," in Germany.
May 14, 1997	Sister Laura Katherine is born to Randy and Lisa Timberlake; she dies shortly after birth.

March 1998–2002	Justin dates singer Britney Spears.
March 24, 1998	*NSYNC is released in the United States.
July 18, 1998	'NSync performs at Disney Concert Special at MGM Studios in Orlando because Backstreet Boys turn down the offer to perform.
August 14, 1998	Brother Stephen Robert is born to Randy and Lisa Timberlake.
October 1998	'NSync tours with Janet Jackson on her Velvet Rope Tour.
November 17, 1998	'NSync's Second II None Tour begins in Orlando; Britney Spears performs as the opening act.
August 1999	'NSync Challenge for the Children charity basketball game in Atlanta, Georgia, raises $50,000.
November 24, 1999	Justin performs on Celine Dion All the Way with 'NSync.
December 1999	'NSync and manager Lou Pearlman head to court over contract agreement.
December 1, 1999	With 'NSync, Justin performs at Christmas Tree Lighting in Rockefeller Center.
March 2000	The band breaks the Ticketmaster record for most single-day sales for their concert to promote No Strings Attached.
March 12, 2000	Disney Channel movie Model Behavior is released; Timberlake plays Jason Sharpe.
March 21, 2000	No Strings Attached album is released.
May 2000	Britney Spears breaks her silence in an interview with Rolling Stone and reveals that she and Justin are a couple.
May 21, 2000	Justin receives his high school diploma at 'NSync concert in Memphis at Pyramid Arena in front of 20,000 fans.
November 19, 2000	After a concert in St. Louis, Missouri, fan Danielle McGuire accuses Justin of allegedly berating and intimidating her.
December 2000	Justin joins other celebrities in Marie Claire's End Gun Violence Now.

2001   Justin establishes the Justin Timberlake Foundation to bring music into schools.

May 23, 2001   'NSync PopOdyssey Tour begins in Jacksonville, Florida.

July 24, 2001   *Celebrity* album is released.

September 2001   Burglars break into home of Justin and Britney and steal home videos; four teenagers are arrested for the break in.

January 2002   First single, "Bye Bye Bye" is released with Jive Records; Justin plays the Bob Hope Classic in Palm Springs, California.

April 23, 2002   Video of the PopOdyssey Tour is released.

April 28, 2002   Last 'NSync concert is performed in Orlando, Florida.

March 2002   Justin and Britney Spears break off their relationship.

March 26, 2002   The film *Longshot*, also known as *Jack of All Trades* in the United States, is released; Justin plays a valet in the film.

July 2002   Justin is voted Most Eligible Bachelor in America.

August 2002   Justin buys a house in Los Angeles for $8.3 million; he joins Hollywood basketball team with other celebrities; and his first single, "Like I Love You," is released.

September 2002–
December 2002   Justin is linked romantically to actress Alyssa Milano.

November 2002   Justin breaks his foot and has to cancel several concert tours.

November 4, 2002   Justin appears on *20/20* with Barbara Walters to promote his solo album.

November 5, 2002   *Justified* album is released.

December 2002   Justin appears on cover of *The Advocate*, a gay and lesbian magazine.

February 20, 2003   Justin performs at the *Brit Awards*.

March 2003	*Inside Drive: A Novel of Basketball, Life and Love*, written by Justin, is published in the United Kingdom.
April 2003	Justin begins dating actress Cameron Diaz.
May 2003	*Justified* tour opens at Hallam FM Arena in Sheffield.
July 30, 2003	Justin participates in SARS event in Toronto, Canada, with the Rolling Stones.
August 28, 2003	Justin cohosts the MTV *Video Music Awards* with Seann William Scott.
October 2003	Justin appears on *Saturday Night Live*.
February 2004	*Justified* receives Best International Album, and Justin wins award for Best International Male Solo Artist at the *Brit Awards*.
February 1, 2004	Justin performs in the half-time show at Super Bowl XXXVIII with Janet Jackson at Houston's Reliant Stadium in Texas; the phrases *wardrobe malfunction* and *costume reveal* are coined.
February 8, 2004	Justin wins Grammy Awards for Best Vocal Album and Best Pop Male.
February 13, 2005	Justin receives a Grammy Award for his philanthropy to the state of Tennessee.
May 5, 2005	Justin has operation for nodules in throat at Cedars Sinai Hospital in Los Angeles.
Summer 2005	Justin founds Jay Tee Records.
August 2005	Justin files charges against British newspaper *News of the World* for a false report of infidelity.
November 2005	Together with Trace Ayala, Justin founds the William Rast clothing line. Clothes become available for sale at Kitson and Bloomingdales.
May 3, 2006	*Promiscuous* video is released featuring Justin, Nelly Furtado, and Timbaland.
July 7, 2006	"SexyBack" song is released.
July 18, 2006	*Edison Force* is released direct to video; Justin plays Josh Pollack in the film.

August 31, 2006 | Justin performs "SexyBack" at the *MTV Video Music Awards*.

September 2006 | Justin is honored with title of King of Pop from *Rolling Stone* magazine.

September 12, 2006 | *FutureSex/LoveSounds* album is released.

December 2006 | Justin breaks up with actress Cameron Diaz; the split is announced on January 11, 2007.

December 5, 2006 | Justin performs "SexyBack" at the Victoria Secret Fashion Show.

January 11, 2007 | Justin performs at a concert in San Jose, California; he announces that he is no longer dating Cameron Diaz.

January 12, 2007 | The film *Alpha Dog* is released; Justin plays gangster Frankie Ballenbacher in the film.

January 15, 2007 | Justin is presented with Best Original Song at the *Golden Globe Awards* in Beverly Hills, California, at Beverly Hilton Hotel.

February 11, 2007 | Justin performs at the *Grammy Awards*.

March 2, 2007 | *Black Snake Moan* is released; Justin plays Ronnie in the film.

March 31, 2007 | Justin hosts Nickelodeon's *Kids' Choice Awards*; he wins the award for Best Male Singer.

April 16, 2007 | Justin tapes Madison Square Garden concert for release on HBO.

May 2007 | Justin founds Tennman Records with Universal Music Group Interscope Geffen A&M.

May 18, 2007 | *Shrek the Third* is released; Justin is the voice of Prince Artie in the film.

June 2007 | Justin is named #2 in *Elle* magazine's "15 Sexiest Men" poll.

June 3, 2007 | Justin is nominated for an MTV Movie Award for *Alpha Dog*.

Summer 2007 | Justin collaborates with Duran Duran on album *Red Carpet Massacre* on the singles "Nite Runner "and "Falling Down."

July 4, 2007   Justin performs concert in London where he proposes a toast to the troops fighting for everyone's freedom.

August 2007   Justin plays a sold-out show in Toronto and Winnipeg, Canada.

August 27, 2007   Justin wins Male Artist, Best Playback Track, and Ultimate Choice Award at the *Teen Choice Awards* and is nominated for Teen Choice Award for Breakout Male Performance in *Alpha Dog*.

November 14, 2007   *Southland Tales* is released; Justin plays Private Pilot Abilene in the film.

December 17, 2007   Justin performs at Philadelphia's Jingle Ball where he debuts the song "4 Minutes," his collaboration with Madonna.

January 8, 2008   Justin is nominated for *People*'s Choice Award for Favorite Star under 35.

February 3, 2008   Justin stars in Pepsi commercial during Super Bowl XLII.

February 7, 2008   Justin participates in *In Style* magazine's "Grammy Salute to Fashion."

February 10, 2008   Justin wins Grammy Award for Best Male Pop Performance and Dance Recording Award.

March 10, 2008   Justin introduces Madonna at Rock and Roll Hall of Fame Banquet in New York.

March 17, 2008   The song "4 Minutes" is released; it is a collaboration with Timberlake, Timbaland, and Madonna.

Spring 2008   Justin produces the NBC show *My Problem with Women*.

June 20, 2008   *The Love Guru* is released; Justin plays Jacques "Le Coq" Grande in the film.

July 2008   The U.S. Court of Appeals for the Third Circuit voids the fine for the Super Bowl incident against CBS.

July 20, 2008   Justin hosts the ESPN *Espy Awards*.

September 5, 2008   Justin performs at Fashion Rocks concert at Radio City Music Hall in New York with proceeds benefiting Stand Up for Cancer.

October 2008	With Leonard DiCaprio, Justin is a part of "Five More Friends" to encourage Americans to vote.
November 2008	"Follow My Lead" single is released.
November 2008	Justin participates in Keep a Child Alive Black Ball, to help the children in Africa.
November 2008	Felipe Ramales, a busboy at the restaurant Southern Hospitality, names Justin in a lawsuit against the restaurant.
November 2008	Justin appears on *Saturday Night Live*.
November 6, 2008	Justin performs "4 Minutes" in Los Angeles with Madonna on her Sticky & Sweet tour at Los Angeles' Dodger Stadium.
November 16, 2008	Justin performs at the finale for MTV's show *Total Request Live*; he dubs *Total Finale Live*.
February 2009	Justin showcases new line of William Rast clothing during New York's Fashion Week.
April 2009	Justin directs and produces television reality series *The Phone*.
Spring 2009	Justin participates in "Summit on the Summit," a climb of Mount Kilimanjaro to raise money for awareness of the water shortage in Africa.
May 2009	Supreme Court sends the Super Bowl fine case back to the U.S. Court of Appeals.
August 28, 2009	*The Open Road* is released; Justin plays Carlton Garrett in the film.
September 2009	Justin participates in celebrity auction for Ten O'Clock Classics; he autographs a grand piano.
September 21, 2009	Justin receives an Emmy Award for *Saturday Night Live*; he is the first *SNL* host to receive such an award.
October 2009	Justin receives a restraining order against alleged stalker Karen J. McNeil.
November 2009	Justin appears in Givenchy commercial for Play perfume.
November 17, 2009	Leona Lewis's album *Echo* is released; Justin writes and sings vocals on "Don't Let Me Down."

December 11, 2009	Justin presents awards at the first annual *Teen-Nick HALO Awards*.
December 15, 2009	Justin announces Golden Globe nominees for 2009.
January 11, 2010	Tennman Records' first-signed artist, Esmee Denters, releases first album, *Outta Here*.
January 15–	
July 17, 2010	Closed Mirimichi Golf Course, Justin's golf course in Tennessee, to make needed improvements.
May 21, 2010	*Shrek Forever After is* released, in which Justin reprises his role as Prince Artie.
October 15, 2010	*The Social Network* is released; Justin plays Sean Parker, Napster president and cofounder of Facebook, in the film.
December 17, 2010	*Yogi Bear* is released; Justin plays Boo-Boo in the film.

CHAPTER 1

A DOWN-HOME BOY

Justin Randall Timberlake was born to Lynn and Randall "Randy" Timberlake on January 31, 1981, in St. Jude Hospital in Memphis, Tennessee. The young couple resided in the small town of Shelby Forest, located to the northwest of Memphis. Although Justin's mother, Lynn, had earned a scholarship to go to college, she opted to get married. At the young age of 17, Lynn Bomar wed the 21-year-old father of Justin, Randy Timberlake, in 1978.

Both Lynn and Randy came from families with musical talent. Lynn's brother played bass in a bluegrass band; it was this band that brought Lynn and Randy together. William Bomar, Lynn's father and Justin's grandfather, was a guitarist and eventually became one of Justin's first music teachers; he taught Justin how to play guitar chords. Bomar used to play informal get-togethers with Elvis Presley. When Justin was old enough to appreciate it, Bomar gave him the guitar he had played while playing with Presley. In an interview with *Billboard* magazine, Justin recounted, "I grew up listening to things that were out on the radio, but also my grandfather taught me about Johnny Cash and Willie Nelson and the importance that they had and how they were ambassadors of country music."[1]

His grandmother "Sadie" Bomar became very attached to the young Justin and would give him peach cobbler whenever he came home to Shelby Forest, Tennessee. Grandma Sadie still sends her blueberry jam, peach cobbler, and squash relish in mason jars to Justin. A retired real estate agent, Grandma Sadie enjoys making her grandson homemade dishes, which he sometimes has to hide on his tour buses so everyone does not eat them. Sadie lives next door to Lynn and her current husband, Paul Harless, in Millington, Tennessee. Justin's grandmother is impressed not only by her grandson's stellar career, but also his manners and belief in God: "I've never seen Justin sit down and eat—even a sandwich—without saying grace first."[2] It is the down-home attitude that Justin learned early in his life that has helped him stay grounded in his career.

From a very early age, Justin seemed to have a passion for music. As a young infant in a car seat, Justin would flail his arms and legs to the beat of the music on the radio. Even when he was placed on the kitchen counter, he would kick his legs to the beat. When he was a toddler, Justin would pretend to play the air guitar when he would unexpectedly join his father on the stage.

The Timberlake legacy comes from England in the 18th century. Lieutenant Henry Timberlake married the daughter of a Cherokee Indian chief when the lieutenant was to negotiate a treaty with the tribe. Charles Timberlake, one of the products of this union, was Randy's father, Justin's grandfather. Charles was the pastor of the Shelby Forest Baptist Church. Randy was an accomplished bluegrass singer. He sang in the choir at the Shelby Forest Church but eventually moved on from the church to make a name for himself. He became a singer and choir director at the Baptist Church in Millington, Tennessee. Justin's father encouraged his son to sing in the church choir. Justin did eventually sing in the church gospel choir, which helped him overcome his shyness of performing in front of people. He became inspired by the "soulful voices of gospel singers."[3]

Randy also exposed Justin to such musical geniuses as the Eagles and Bob Seger. Because of his father, Justin enjoyed the "Bohemian Rhapsody" by Queen. Shelby Forest and Millington, Tennessee, where the Timberlakes raised Justin, were major influences on his musical styles. Memphis is the "home of the blues, birthplace of rock, and the capital of soul."⁴ Memphis was also the home of gospel, Elvis, and the Gibson guitar plant. Millington had a number of different musical clubs of many different styles. Ike Turner, B. B. King, and Howlin' Wolf also started their musical careers there. During his early years, Justin took to the blues of Memphis and looked into learning more about its roots. It was not only the lyrics that Justin was enamored by, it was also the melodies and harmonies. As a child, Justin would lock himself in his room to listen to and learn the exact melodies and harmonies of songs.

At the age of four, Justin's parents divorced in 1985. Despite the divorce, Justin remains close to both of his biological parents. Lynn's mother, Sadie, helped raise Justin after the divorce. Bill Bomar, in building his house, also built a place on his property for Lynn and Justin. Because Lynn was young when Justin was born, she always felt she was growing up with Justin.

Lynn was working at First Tennessee National Corporation bank when she met fellow banker, Paul Harless. Lynn's relationship with Paul blossomed, and he and Lynn were married when Justin was just five years old. Harless became a very important part of Justin's life. Justin's sense of humor and demeanor came from Harless. Harless has also instilled in Justin the need for a strong family. Discipline was also a strong suit with Harless. When Justin wanted to get his ears pierced at the age of 13, Harless told him he had to earn the privilege. Justin was to write a song and perform it in front of the family. "The Earring Song" was written, and Justin sang the song in front of the family while they were on vacation in Hawaii. There was a fun side to Harless as well, teaching Justin how to play golf when he was only 10 years old. Harless has shared Justin's love for golf throughout his life and also participates in the same charity tournaments as his stepson.

Justin's father, Randy, also remarried. He married Lisa Perry. Lisa worked at Lebonheur Children's Hospital in Memphis and at Shelby Forest Church. She is a pharmacist, pianist, and a horsewoman. During her high school years, Lisa won the Tennessee High School Rodeo Association Breakaway Roping and Goat Tying Championship. Randy and Lisa had three children together. Jonathan Perry was born September 12, 1993. Laura Katherine was born May 14, 1997, but died shortly after birth. Justin mentions his half sister in the *NSYNC album acknowledgments and refers to her as "My Angel in Heaven." Stephen

Robert was born August 14, 1998. Both of his half brothers have added generously to Justin's life.

Lisa's parents, Mack and Mimi, have also added to Justin's life. "Pa Mack," who lives with Randy and Lisa, has a great singing voice and is part of the quartet at Shelby Forest Baptist Church. He is an inspiration to Justin. Mimi taught Justin to ride horses when he was eight years old. She bought him a pony named Molly. Unfortunately, the horse developed founder, a painful inflammation of the hind and front feet. The disease also restricts the movement of the animal. Fortunately, Justin was involved in other activities, including basketball and singing, so it kept his mind off his ailing pony.

Although his parents divorced when he was young, Justin had the opportunity to grow up in a very loving and supportive extended family. His life is also grounded in his strong belief in God. While he was growing up, he attended church with both his grandfather and his father. Although his grandfather was a Baptist minister, Justin does not practice any certain form of religion. He was raised Baptist but "considers himself to be more spiritual than religious."[5] Justin said, "My thing is that God is all around us in everything we say, everything we do, everything we feel. I really believe that."[6]

Justin credits his mother, Lynn, with becoming the person he is today. Justin was a very shy child and would walk around with his head down most of the time. Lynn realized that he had talent when he was very young and worked to extract the talent from her shy son. Lynn knows what to expect from her son and has ambitions for him to succeed but also realizes that even Justin has limitations. According to his mother, "He always got out of the bed on the wrong side, however, and he is a legend in his own household for being completely antisocial for the first hour of the day and ready to bite Lynn's head off if she talked to him."[7] Justin is also a perfectionist who at times exhibits a temper. Lynn said that "he (Justin) can be moody, mostly when it comes to his work."[8] She has encouraged his singing career and, as a daredevil herself, his love of motorcycles. When Justin received his first paycheck from his first album with 'NSync, he bought his mother a Harley Davidson, placing the keys in a jewelry box. He also has a tattoo on his back of an angel with his mother's initials, referencing his mother as his guardian angel.

Lynn has also developed a managing company for musicians. She put together Innosense, the girl band equivalent to 'NSync. The group included Nikki DeLoach, Danay Ferrer, Mandy Ashford, and Amanda Latona. Both she and Paul Harless manage Just In Time Entertainment. The two split their time between Shelby Forest and Orlando, Florida.

Justin's elementary school also shaped his personality and his career aspirations. E. E. Jeter Elementary School, the only school Justin ever attended, was named after Squire Emmett Early Jeter in 1923 and is one of the oldest schools in Shelby County. During his years at E. E. Jeter, Justin was called "Curly" and "Brillo" because his hair was so curly. He cut his hair in second grade but got in trouble for doing so by his mother. The only other time he got in trouble in school was when he put braids in his hair. His punishment was to copy part of the dictionary. He was also called pizza face in junior high because of his acne. Despite the name calling, Justin was a well-liked child. He would constantly look down at his sneakers during his preteen years, which his mother believed led to his love of sneakers later on in his life. Justin now owns more than 500 pairs of sneakers. Basketball was a big part of Justin's school life. He joined the algebra club but quit because it interfered with basketball. He also was in the talent shows and maintained As throughout his school career. His accolades during his time at E. E. Jeter Elementary included spelling bee champion.

Several people at E. E. Jeter influenced Justin as well. Seventh-grade teacher Renee Earnest always encouraged Justin's talents. She believed he always had a good sense of humor and comedic talent. Principals Mary Ann McNeil and Regina Castleberry found Justin to be a talented individual. Despite his gifts, Justin was a typical teenager who did not know where his life was going. At the GMTV Europe's TV Network, he talked about his elementary school days, commenting, "I had really awkward hair and terrible skin, and I was really scrawny."[9]

Like any other young boy, Justin had his disappointments. During his last year at E. E. Jeter, his dog Scooter ran away. When he was finally found, Scooter had to be put down because he ate poison. Lynn's terrier, Ozzie, named because he looked like Toto in *The Wizard of Oz*, did not like Justin. The two of them did not get along, and Ozzie constantly nipped at Justin's ankles. Lynn also gave up her pet cat, Millie, went she went to Orlando to be with 'NSync. The cat went to Chuck and Sherry Yerger, one of Justin's mentors and his wife.

Justin did not let his insecurities hold him back. Justin's first kiss was when he was 10 years old to 11-year-old Mindy Mabry. At the homecoming dance, he and his date, Deanna Dooley, were named Mr. and Ms. Jeter. His best friend, Trace Ayala, helped him through the awkward times too. Born Juan Trace Ayala III, Ayala was born November 26, 1980, in Memphis, Tennessee. Ayala and Justin grew up together because their mothers were best friends. They shared a similar sense of humor and vacationed together. Ayala dropped out of school to tour with 'NSync. His tattoo, "Space Cowboy," is in memory of 'NSync's first tour. He is now known as Justin's personal assistant and lives in the guest house on Justin's Los Angeles property. He was engaged to actress Elisha Cuthbert in June 2004. Cuthbert was Justin's friend before becoming friends with Ayala. Justin and Cuthbert were rumored to be dating because the two had been seen together, but in reality, it was Cuthbert and Ayala who were dating. Ayala was also engaged to Joanna Garcia in 2008, but he broke off the engagement in August 2009.

Justin gets back home whenever he can for his Grandmother Sadie's peach cobbler. He also enjoys philly cheesesteak sandwiches and home-cooked fries. He comes back to help out his former school with whatever he can because he has the means and opportunity. In an interview with *Rolling Stone*, he commented, "I grew up in the boondocks, and there just wasn't a good musical program at school. I've thought about it a little bit—this and the whole Columbine incident. Music is another way for young minds and young bodies to express themselves, to find a way to get all these negative thoughts and energies out."[10]

In an effort to honor Justin for his many contributions to the state of Tennessee, State Senator Ophelia Ford wanted the legislature to officially honor him for his "highly successful music career and for his meritorious service to the state of Tennessee."[11] Other senators, however, were opposed to the resolution, so it did not pass in 2007.

Growing up in a stable and supportive environment formed Justin into the musical genius he is today. He has learned how to take his successes and failures in stride and build on them for future success. The building blocks of his character came from Justin's roots in Tennessee.

NOTES

1. Hal Marcovitz, *Justin Timberlake: A View from the Paparazzi* (Broomall, PA: Mason Crest Publishers, 2008), p. 14.

2. Michelle Tauber, "Justin Timberlake," *People*, June 24, 2005, http://www.people.com.

3. James DeMedeiros, *Justin Timberlake: Remarkable People Series* (New York: Weigl Publishers, 2009), p. 6.

4. Holly Cefry, *Justin Timberlake: Contemporary Musicians and Their Music* (New York: Rosen Publishing, 2009), p. 7.

5. "'NSync Discusses Their Rise to Stardom," *Larry King Live*, January 9, 2001, http://www.cnn.com.

6. Sean Smith, *Justin: The Unauthorized Biography* (New York: Pocket Books, 2004), p. 34.

7. Ibid., p. 42.

8. Tauber, "Justin Timberlake."

9. Steve Dougherty, *Justin Timberlake: Junk Food Tasty Celebrity Bios* (New York: Scholastic, 2009), p. 19.

10. Marcovitz, *Justin Timberlake*, p. 53.

11. "Tennessee Officials Split over Timberlake Honor," *World Entertainment News Network*, March 23, 2007, www.wenn.com.

CHAPTER 2

THE BEGINNING OF A CAREER

With good looks and a good feel for music, Justin was pursuing his musical dream at a very young age. By two years old, he was singing harmonies of songs on the radio. At the young age of eight, Justin demonstrated excellent pitch and the confidence to perform in front of an audience. In an interview with *Time for Kids*, Justin said, "Ever since I was a really little boy I always sang. So I figured out that that was sort of my calling. I didn't really have to think about it because I knew it was always there, that it's what I should be doing."[1] Support and encouragement from his family also helped.

Many genres of music have shaped Justin's musical talent, such as rhythm and blues, rock and roll, country, and gospel music. Justin has listened to and enjoyed the likes of Marvin Gaye, Al Green, Stevie Wonder, and Donny Hathaway. He has listed his favorite songwriter as John Lennon and his favorite album is Michael Jackson's *Off the Wall*. He has been influenced by the bands Strokes, Killers, Arcade Fire, Radiohead, and Coldplay. Justin also cites his hometown as giving him musical talent: "The many sounds of Memphis shaped my early musical career and continue to be an inspiration to this day."[2]

E. E. Jeter Elementary School gave Justin the opportunity to practice in front of an audience. In the third grade, he and his friends lip synched to one of the songs from New Kids on the Block, a popular boy band of the 1980s. While Justin sang and his friends lip-synched, the crowd was impressed. Among those taping the performance was Justin's mother, Lynn. She saw his potential and sent him to Bob Westbrook, a singing coach. Lynn had also taken voice lessons from Westbrook.

During his time with Westbrook, Justin joined his troupe, the Bob Westbrook Singers. The group, made up of six girls and Justin, performed at a variety of local events. They were also entered in several talent contests. At the Mid South State Faire, the singers made it to the finals with Holly Gaines headlining the song "More Than Wonderful."

By the age of 10, Justin was looking for ways to get himself noticed as a singer. He sang for a charity event at the Grand Ole Opry. On August 8, 1992, he won the Universal Charm Pageant. As the only male contestant, Justin sang Percy Sledge's song, "When a Man Loves a Woman." The five accolades he won were for Best Model, Best Dressed, Best Sportswear, Most Handsome, and Supreme Winner. His reward for winning the contest was $16,000 in U.S. savings bonds.

In 1992 Justin also tried out for *Star Search*. This was a popular show in the 1990s hosted by Ed McMahon. Contestants performed in front of judges to receive stars to win the competition. Several other celebrities who attribute *Star Search* as helping them in their early careers include Britney Spears, Beyonce, Christina Aguilera, LeAnn Rimes, Alanis Morissette, and Rosie O'Donnell. Justin was chosen to perform among 500 who auditioned for the junior vocalist competition. The prize for winning was $25,000. He sang Garth Brooks's "Two of a Kind." To add to the song, he wore a bolo tie, a cowboy hat, and a western shirt. He won a spot on the show. For the final run to win the show, he sang Alan Jackson's "Love's Got a Hold on You." Justin received three and a quarter stars but lost the competition to a 10-year-old girl, Anna Nardona, who received four stars. She sang "Don't It Make My Brown Eyes Blue" by Crystal Gayle.

The upside to losing the *Star Search* competition was that Justin was more determined to make it as a superstar. He credits losing on *Star Search* as the stepping stone to auditioning for *The All-New Mickey*

Mouse Club. If he had won the *Star Search* competition, he would not have had the time or opportunity to audition. Justin was quoted as saying, "It's funny. If I had won on *Star Search* just one time, I would not have made the audition. I think God has his master plan and he'll lay it out for you. But you have to walk that road."[3]

Justin auditioned for *The All-New Mickey Mouse Club* in 1993. He was already a fan of Disney's *Captain EO* show, the 17-minute, 3-D film with Michael Jackson. Justin saw the show, produced by *Star Wars* director George Lucas, more than 20 times. Cast members were between the ages of 11 and 18 years old, and the show itself was aimed at an older crowd than the previous Mickey Mouse shows. More than 20,000 adolescents tried out for *The All-New Mickey Mouse Club.* Gary Spatz auditioned Justin on six main aspects including appearance, personality, confidence, dancing, acting, and vocals. Justin sang "When a Man Loves a Woman." Spatz was excited about the passion and drive Justin displayed during his audition. He was paid $15,000 for the six-month season that included 35 episodes that ran from April to September. Six other people joined the ranks of *The All-New Mickey Mouse Club* including Britney Spears, Christina Aguilera, Ryan Gosling, Tate Lynche, Nikki DeLoach, and TJ Fantini. Jessica Simpson and Matt Damon also tried out for the sixth season but did not make the cut. Both Spears and Aguilera auditioned for *Star Search* but failed to get into the competition.

At the age of 11, Justin moved to Orlando, Florida, to perform on *The All-New Mickey Mouse Club.* He and his mother, Lynn, lived away from Tennessee for six months while he taped the show. The singer would leave his ordinary life at E. E. Jeter, his friends, and his family to perform on the show. Aside from being away from home, Justin's mother was concerned about his naming credits. The name chosen would be with him for the rest of his life. Lynn's choices were "Justin Randall Timberlake," "Justin Randall," "Justin Timberlake," or "Randall Timberlake," after his father. Justin made the ultimate decision to stick with "Justin Timberlake." Although he would miss his life in Tennessee, Justin felt comfortable in a place where there were other kids who enjoyed performing and singing as much as he did.

The experience on the Disney show was invaluable to Justin's early career. The show mixed comedy sketches with current musical hits.

An ongoing soap opera, called *Emerald Cove,* also brought the show success with the teenage set. Another popular segment of the show was when the profiles of the young actors of the cast were revealed. During Justin's profile, he introduced the audience to Memphis, Tennessee. He did Elvis impersonations and invited his friends to join him. He showed the viewers Graceland and the trolley. Filmed before a live audience at Disney's MGM Studios (which today is called Hollywood Studios), the celebrities learned how to perform in front of an audience. They learned about different musical styles, sounds, and harmonies. Justin was asked to sing R&B by producer Robin Wiley. The teens also learned how to act as part of a group rather than always looking for the spotlight. "He had his share of moments on stage, but also sang backup for the other performers. He learned how to perform as part of a group, not just as the center of attention," producer Wiley said.[4]

The actors and actresses never wore the Mickey Mouse ears as the stars did on previous versions of the show in the 1950s and 1970s. Theme shows were also popular with the 1990s version of the Mickey Mouse Club. Mondays were typically Music Day, Guest Day was on Tuesdays, Anything Can Happen Day! was on Wednesdays, Thursdays were Party Day! and Friday was Hall of Fame Day. In season seven, the last season of the show, theme days were nonexistent because the show only aired on Thursdays.

The All-New Mickey Mouse Club was also the place where Justin and Britney Spears first met. Spears was born December 2, 1981, in McComb, Mississippi, and raised in Kentwood, Louisiana. She grew up with similar Southern musical influences as Justin and was raised Southern Baptist. Spears began her performing career in gymnastics and singing in the church choir. When she was eight years old, she attended the Professional Performing Arts school in New York City. In 2002 her parents divorced. It was also at the age of eight that she auditioned for the first time for *The All-New Mickey Mouse Club.* At the time, the Disney executives thought she was too small for a role on the show but turned her on to a New York agent. She continued to go to the Professional Performing Arts school and was cast in several off-Broadway shows while she was in New York. In 1992 Spears was on the show *Star Search* but, like Justin, did not win. Their paths to fame have been very similar. At the age of 11, she returned to audition for the show and finally was given a spot. She was on the show from 1993 to 1994. After the show was cancelled in 1994, Spears spent a stint in the girl band Innosense, the band that Justin's mother had managed. On *The All-New Mickey Mouse Club*, Justin and Spears did a duet of the song "I Feel For You." Justin was enamored with her immediately. The couple dated until they were 21 years old. "I was in love with her from the start. I was infatuated with her from the start," Justin said in an interview with *Gentleman's Quarterly*.[5]

Because the children on *The All-New Mickey Mouse Club* needed to go to school sometime during their daily routine, Disney executives hired tutors for the set. The Screen Actors Guild (SAG) and the American Federation of Television and Radio Actors (AFTRA) required child actors to be in school three hours a day or 15 hours a week. The children's course work had to be approved first with the celebrity's school back home. A typical day started with the bus picking the children up at 7 A.M. to bring them to the school located on the lot. The cast would have three hours of schooling followed by rehearsals all afternoon. Homework was also assigned to be turned in the next day. The rigorous schedule kept the children disciplined. Because of the demanding schedule of schooling and the show, the children had little time to themselves. During free time, the children were allowed to go out for ice cream. They would also use their Silver Passports, free tickets to get them into Walt Disney World theme parks.

The show aired Monday–Thursday in the 5:30 time slot during season six. In the final season, the show only aired on Thursday evenings at 7:30. In 1994 production of the show was cancelled, but Disney ran reruns of the show up until May 1996. Many of the young actors and actresses on the show in the 1990s went on to become musicians and singers in their own right. Britney Spears and Christina Aguilera now have successful music careers. Ryan Gosling has a promising career as an actor in such films as *The Notebook* and *Half Nelson*. JC Chasez went on to sing in the boy band 'NSync with Justin.

Going back to Tennessee after the show was cancelled gave Justin more confidence in his singing and dancing skills. He felt more comfortable resuming his schooling at E. E. Jeter after his celebrity on *The All-New Mickey Mouse Club* because he had been with the same classmates since kindergarten. He sang many solos in musicals at E. E. Jeter. He also sang at the home of Mrs. Castleberry, E. E. Jeter's principal, when she conducted Alpha Delta Kappa (ADK) sorority meetings. ADK sorority is a social club that met for dinner, discussions, and entertainment. Justin also performed at a Millington School carnival, again singing Garth Brooks. Debbie Welch, the carnival's organizer, was unsure about Justin's dance moves in front of the 300 spectators. He had never had any professional dance lessons, and Welch made sure it would not be too risqué for the town of Millington. Fortunately, his dance moves did not offend anyone at all.

The next step of Justin's career took him back to his Mouseketeer days. JC Chasez, who had been on *The All-New Mickey Mouse Club* for four years before it was cancelled, was interested in singing with Justin. Neither of the boys was ready to give up the fame they had felt on *The All-New Mickey Mouse Club*. They also did not want to stop performing. The two went to Nashville in pursuit of a record contract with the demo they paid to have recorded. Shortly thereafter, the two boys, who had once been heartthrobs on *The All-New Mickey Mouse Club*, became four boys the world would eventually fawn over.

NOTES

1. Jillian Klueber, "Justin's Solo Act," *Time for Kids*, November 11, 2002, http://www.timeforkids.com/TFK/kids/news/kidscoops/.

2. James DeMedeiros, *Justin Timberlake: Remarkable People Series* (New York: Weigl Publishers, 2009), p. 11.

3. Sean Smith, *Justin: The Unauthorized Biography* (New York: Pocket Books, 2004), p. 52.

4. Terri Dougherty, *Justin Timberlake: People in the News* (Farmington Hills, MI: Lucent Books, 2008), p. 20.

5. Lisa DePaulo, "Locked and Loaded," *Gentlemen's Quarterly*, August 2006, p. 116.

CHAPTER 3

'NSYNC

Justin's break into the boy band scene came after his stint with *The All-New Mickey Mouse Club*. After returning home to Tennessee when the show was cancelled, Justin was not there long when he was asked by fellow Mouseketeer JC Chasez to start a band. He and Chasez made a demo tape in Nashville and worked on getting a music contract. Boy bands New Kids on the Block and Backstreet Boys paved the way for boy bands in the pop music genre. "The term (boy band) usually refers to a group of young male singers who perform pop music. They often sing in harmony and perform elaborate moves," according to author Tony Napoli.[1] The shelf-life of a boy band is approximately five years, but 'NSync would surpass that statistic.

JC Chasez was born Joshua Scott Chasez on August 8, 1976, in Washington D.C. When Chasez was five years old, he was adopted by Roy and Karen Chasez. His biological mother gave her son to her foster parents to ensure that her son would have a good life and an education. Chasez became good friends with Justin when the two were on *The All-New Mickey Mouse Club*. Chasez was the show's front man for the last two seasons of the show. He had been on the show for a total of five seasons. During spare moments of the show, he sang with vocal coach

Robin Wiley or attended dancing classes to hone his skills. After *The All-New Mickey Mouse Club*, Chasez returned to Baltimore. He was working in a restaurant when he finally returned to Orlando to join the boy band. As a strict music man, he likes to write songs and has to be constantly moving and performing. He shared Justin's trait of being a perfectionist. When 'NSync went their separate ways, Chasez was in the movies *Killer Movie, 21 and a Wake-up*, and *Kerosene Cowboys*. He also had a dream of recording solo albums. His first solo album, *Schizophrenia*, was released February 24, 2004. He also wrote "Treat Me Right" for the Backstreet Boys in 2007, which is featured on the group's album *Unbreakable*.

'NSync is unique in that all the members were found through friends and referrals. This eliminated some of the competition in holding auditions for other members of the band. The members worked with vocal coaches and writers and put together a demo.

Christopher Kirkpatrick was found performing at Universal Studios in Orlando. He was singing with a doo-wop group called the Hollywood Hi-Tones. He had originally auditioned with the Backstreet Boys. Kirkpatrick was born on October 17, 1971, in Clarion, Pennsylvania. He came from Pennsylvania and had many musical connections. He was known as a class clown and was very interested in performing in front of an audience. During school, he performed in *Oliver* and *South Pacific*, as well as other plays and talent contests. Eventually, he graduated from Valencia College with an associate of arts degree. He learned to play the guitar, keyboards, and trombone. Not immune to working hard to make money, Kirkpatrick's jobs included picking up sheep feces at the age of 13, working in a grocery store from 4 A.M. to 8 A.M. before school, and being a waiter at Outback Steakhouse. After 'NSync stopped singing together, he decided to pursue acting. He was in a new band called Little Red Monsters. Also to his credit was a voice-over bit for the cartoon show *The Fairly Odd Parents*. Fuman Skeeto was Kirkpatrick's clothing line, which closed. As with any boy band, the admiring girls were a large part of the scene. However, Kirkpatrick was only interested in artistic girls. He was into women who were lively, like Cheri Oteri from *Saturday Night Live*.

Joey Fatone was also interested in forming a boy band. Fatone met Kirkpatrick when he was also performing at Universal Studios. He portrayed Wolfie Werewolf in *The Beetlejuice Graveyard Revue*. Both his brother, Steven, and his sister, Janine, worked at Universal Studios. Fatone was born January 28, 1977, in Bensonhurst, Brooklyn, New York. His musical influences include Boys II Men and his father. His father, Joseph Fatone, Sr., was a member of the Orions, who performed songs from the 1950s and 1960s. During school, Fatone was in many plays and musicals. At the age of 13, he went from New York to Florida to try out for *The All-New Mickey Mouse Club*. He did not make the cut for the show. Fatone was working at Universal Studios when he was asked to be in 'NSync. He always wanted to be an actor rather than a singer. After 'NSync, he was in *On the Line*, with fellow band member Lance Bass, and *My Big Fat Greek Wedding*. His other acting credits include *Matinee, Once Upon a Time in America,* and the television show *Sea Quest*. He also performed on Broadway in *Little Shop of Horrors* and *Rent* in 2003. In 2007 he was a contestant on *Dancing with the Stars* with his partner Kym Johnson. Personally, Fatone has a daughter Brianna with Kelly Baldwin. He also has a large Superman collection and a quirky fashion sense.

Charles Edward was the next one invited to join 'NSync. He had originally sung with the Backstreet Boys but was asked to leave the band. He continued working on his singing, taking voice lessons, and eventually joined 'NSync. He left shortly after the band began to get married. He was then replaced by Jason Galasso, who was working at Flipper's Pizza.

With the five members of the band together, Justin, Kirkpatrick, Chasez, Fatone, and Galasso, the band was ready to start producing. Justin's mother, Lynn, was the appointed den mother for the group in their Orlando home on Doctor Phillips Boulevard. It is also said that Lynn originated the band's name using the last letter in each of the singer's name—JustiN, ChriS, JoeY, JasoN, and JC. Shortly into the band's formation Galasso believed that 'NSync was not a happening band and quit. Justin looked to his Nashville singing coach, Bob Westerbrook, for a replacement. The solution was singer Lance Bass, whose full name was Lansten so the origination of 'NSync's name still worked with the last letter of everyone's name.

Bass was born James Lansten Bass in Laurel, Mississippi, on May 4, 1979. His mother was a teacher, and his father worked for the local

phone company. With a Christian upbringing like Justin, the two became friends. He was a member of the music venue Mississippi Show
Stoppers. He was influenced by Garth Brooks at the age of 14. Together
with his mother, Diane, he traveled to Orlando to be in 'NSync. His
mother was skeptical of the whole opportunity. Bass was enrolled in the
University of Nebraska home-school program. Bass is very involved
with his career, and after singing with 'NSync, he became involved in
acting. His dream had always been to travel to outer space. He applied
to join the shuttle launch with the Russian Space Agency. His goal was
to be the first rock star in space, but he did not achieve his goal because
he could not find financial backing. Bass's acting credits include voice-
overs in such cartoon comedies as *Kim Possible* and *Robot Chicken*. He
also has his own managing company, called A Happy Place, and has
signed such singers as Meredith Edwards. His film production company, Bacon and Eggs, has turned out the films *Lovewrecked* and his
own movie *On The Line*.

In 2006 Bass told the world in a magazine article that he was gay and
dating *The Amazing Race* reality star Reichen Lehmkuhl. He was afraid
of revealing his homosexuality during 'NSync because he didn't want it
to negatively affect the boy band's popularity. In an interview with *People*
magazine, he said, "I knew that I was in this popular band and I had four
other guys' careers in my hand, and I knew that if I ever acted on it or
even said (that I was gay), it would overpower everything. I didn't know.
Could that be the end of 'NSync? So I had that weight on me of 'Wow,
if I ever let anyone know, it's bad.' So I just never did."[2] Despite his waiting to tell the world that he was homosexual until 2006, his former band
members were very supportive of their friend. Fatone told *People* magazine that he knew it was hard for Bass to figure out how to tell everyone,
and Justin wished his former band mate all the happiness in the world.

In October of 2007, Bass's biography *Out of Sync: A Memoir* was
published by Simon Spotlight Entertainment, a division of Simon &
Schuster. In the biography, Bass talks about his relationship with all five
of his band mates as well as his time with 'NSync. He speaks frankly
about the break up of the band and about why he did not feel he could
tell anyone at that time that he was gay. Bass was also friends and greatly
influenced by Michael Jackson. He credits some of 'NSync's success to
Jackson as the band emulated and copied some of his dance moves.

Jackson also supported Bass in his career aspirations. When Jackson died in 2009, Bass commented in an *MTV News* article, "I am stunned and deeply saddened by the sudden loss of Michael Jackson. Michael was a huge supporter of my career, but more importantly he was a good friend, had the biggest heart, and it was an honor and pleasure to be able to work with him and know him. There will never be another Michael Jackson. My thoughts and prayers are with his family."[3]

The band members had to take day jobs to support themselves and then would practice into the wee hours of the morning. Although the group was tired, they knew what they had to do to succeed. Justin commented, "We didn't take it lightly. We knew what we wanted and we concentrated on it."[4]

With the members of the band in place, the crew signed with Lou Pearlman, known in the industry as Big Poppa. He grew up with music and began playing guitar at the age of eight. He received an MBA from Queens College. His musical credits include being a member of a rock and soul band that played with both Donna Summer and Kool and the Gang. Pearlman composed "Just Another Lonely Night." He also managed the Backstreet Boys. He owned an aviation business that helped get his band where they needed to go for concerts.

Pearlman helped the band financially. He also hired choreographers, vocal coaches, public relations specialists, image stylists, songwriters, producers, and studio musicians to help the band succeed. Pearlman hired Johnny Wright as their manager, who also was the manager for Backstreet Boys, and started out as a driver for New Kids on the Block. Choreographer Tony Michaels helped the band. His prodigies included Jennifer Lopez and the Christian girl band Zoe Girl. They worked with famous producers such as Rodney Jenkins, Brian McKnight, Pharrell Williams, and The Neptunes. He called his hard regimen O Town boot camp, where the band members would learn all the harmonies and dance moves in his studio. He had the band doing Coca-Cola and Pepsi commercials. The group had their first public performance at Pleasure Island at Walt Disney World in Orlando on October 22, 1995. The Backstreet Boys became upset after 'NSync signed with Pearlman because they thought they were being pushed aside for a newer boy band. Pearlman's vision was to make the boy band popular before they were introduced to the United States.

In 1999 ABC filmed a documentary series with Pearlman on how teen bands can make it big. It was based on the reality-type shows that started out first by doing teen auditions to find a new group for Pearlman to mold into a success. He used the same venues he used to make 'NSync and the Backstreet Boys a success. The band was also housed in Orlando, the same way 'NSync was at the beginning of the formation of the band.

Pearlman got a record deal for 'NSync with BMG Records in Europe. In October 1996, the band's first single, "I Want You Back," was released in Germany. They promoted their band by playing coffeehouses, pubs, and colleges. 'NSync was the opening act in Germany for DJ Bobo. They sang "Everything I Own" by David Gates and "Sailing" by Christopher Cross. Their first accolade was being awarded Best Newcomer of the Year by a German magazine. The single first reached number one in Sweden and within weeks became the number one song across the continent. Between October 7 and November 9, 1996, the band did 30 shows. The second single, "Tearin' Up My Heart," was written by Max Martin and Kristian Lundin. It was featured as song number 30 on VH1's special *100 Greatest Songs of the 90s*.

During the time that their singles were coming out, Justin was learning how to capture and retain the audience's attention. Although he learned a lot during his childhood about performing in front of an audience, he was interested in honing his dance moves. Justin worked with Max Martin and Denniz Pop to learn dance moves. When Pop died in 1998 of cancer, his apprentice Max Martin took over completely.

With everything going right for the band, they released their first album, *NSYNC, in Germany. Pearlman believed that breaking into the music industry in the United States would be easier if they found a following overseas first. Many of Pearlman's bands took this route. The album sold more than 250,000 copies. In an interview with *Billboard* magazine, Justin commented, "We're not just a recording group, we're friends. We're growing and changing and making music that is real and honest . . . As long as we continue to remain true to who we are, we have a fair shot at being heard. That's all we've every really wanted: to be heard."[5] After touring Europe and performing in bands and coffeehouses, 'NSync was making a fan base.

Pearlman realized the band was ready to debut in the United States. The band's first single released in America was "I Want You Back" on January 20, 1998. He landed a contract with RCA Records for 'NSync. On March 24, 1998, *NSYNC was released in the United States. The album released in the United States had bonus tracks. In August 1998, a quarter of a million copies had been sold in the span of five days and had reached number one on *Billboard* charts. In six months, the *NSYNC album reached platinum status, selling more than one million copies. The album spawned four number-one hits, including "I Want You Back," "Tearin' Up My Heart," "God Must Have Spent a Little More Time on You," and "Drive Myself Crazy." Eminem did a parody of "Tearin' Up My Heart" titled "Tearin' Up My Ass." To commemorate the success of the album, the band members, except Joey Fatone, got tattoos. Justin's was a flame tattoo on his ankle.

The band's music was enough to attract fans, but they were also interested in the style that 'NSync brought to the table. The group would wear T-shirts and skinny jeans, and they had earrings. It was not uncommon for teenagers to try and emulate the dress of the members of 'NSync.

'NSync played concerts on radio stations and in malls to promote their music. On July 19, 1998, 'NSync performed at Disney's Summer Concert Series in Orlando at MGM Studios after the Backstreet Boys backed out of the engagement. The concert series increased the sales of the new album. The band also participated in Disney's Holiday Concert and Disney's Christmas Parade. They continued their promotion in October 1998 when they sang with Janet Jackson on her Velvet Rope Tour. 'NSync and Jackson sang an a cappella version of Stevie Wonder's song "Overjoyed." The band toured in 1998 and had singer Britney Spears as the opening act.

'NSync released its second album, *Home for Christmas*, at the end of 1998. The album featured the songs "The First Noel," "Holy Night," "Will You Be Mine for Christmas?" and "In Love on Christmas." With the release of this new album, 'NSync now had two albums on the *Billboard* Top 10. The album sold more than four million copies. It featured Justin singing an "O Holy Night" solo. Two of the songs that were recorded during the making of *Home for Christmas* did not make it on the album. "I Don't Want to Spend One More Christmas without You" debuted on the *Now That's What I Call Christmas, Volume II*, and "You Don't Have to Be Alone on Christmas" can be found on *The Grinch* soundtrack.

With the release of these two albums and the concerts they performed, they were heading into the top of all the U.S. music charts. Despite the high rate of success, critics were saying 'NSync was selling their songs because of their style and looks instead of real talent. The choreographed acts in their concerts gave something audiences could watch as well as to listen to. Fans would go to great lengths to see the band while they were on the road. People would try to sneak into their hotel rooms. While overseas in Europe, fans would chase their buses for miles at a time. In the United States, fans held signs and screamed when the boy band premiered in Times Square for MTV's *Total Request Live*. One such fan was Gabby Sidibe, who now is an aspiring actress herself and has starred in the movie *Precious*. She had seen 'NSync in concert 23 times and was present for the Times Square performance. Sibide said, "I was holding a sign . . . Justin's birthday is January 31st and Joey's birthday is the 28th and we were holding this sign: Please let us up to say happy birthday to Joey and Justin.' That's how fanatical I was."[6]

The band had made their mark on the music industry by performing at the *Academy Awards*, the World Series, and the Olympics. They had worked with such musicians as Britney Spears, Aerosmith, Michael Jackson, Celine Dion, Janet Jackson, and Stevie Wonder. 'NSync was featured on *The Simpsons* and *Saturday Night Live*. On *Saturday Night Live*, the band did a skit as 7 Degrees Celsius. In 1999, 'NSync performed on the television show *Sabrina and the Teenage Witch*. The group sang "Tearin' Up My Heart" and "God Must Have Spent a Little More Time on You." The boys also performed at the Grand Ole Opry House on September 22, 1999, at the 33rd annual *Country Music Association Awards*. They performed the song "God Must Have Spent a Little More Time on You" with Alabama. The song is featured on Alabama's *Twentieth Century* album. Before the performance, Bass was the only member of 'NSync who was into country music. After agreeing to the performance at the Grand Ole Opry, Bass made his fellow band mates listen to it. In an interview Bass said, "The other guys weren't into country at all, but since I've made them listen to it, they actually respect and enjoy a lot of it."[7]

To attract more fans, the group appeared on *The View, The Tonight Show with Jay Leno,* and the *Rosie O'Donnell Show.* After the *Rosie O'Donnell Show,* there was a charity auction for the chairs in which the band members sat. Justin's chair brought in the most money for the charity auction. The group was featured on many magazine covers, including *Rolling Stone* and *Entertainment Weekly.* The phenomenon that was 'NSync was sweeping the world much to the chagrin of other boy bands like Backstreet Boys, Boys II Men, 98 Degrees, and Hanson.

During the summer of 2000, 'NSync used their celebrity for a good cause. The band auctioned off tickets to one of their concerts. The package included four tickets to a concert and a pass to interact with the band before or after the show. The minimum bid was $500. The auction benefited the Justin Timberlake Foundation and 'NSync's Challenge for the Children.

Aside from the music, 'NSync soon became an industry itself. There were 'NSync T-shirts, hats, and dolls. The web site became the most popular in the world with one million hits a month.[8] The band had to wear ear pieces because the screaming at their concerts was so loud. Across the world, the islands of St. Vincent and Grenadines had 'NSync featured on postage stamps. This is an honor as most countries only depict dead people on their postage stamps. Justin was also becoming more popular because of his relationship with Britney Spears. He became the center of attention in newspapers, magazines, and the tabloids. They would follow the prominent singers wherever they went.

'NSync was invited to sing "The Star Spangled Banner" at Super Bowl XXXV. The New York Giants played the Baltimore Ravens. Ray Charles and Aerosmith were also musical guests at the sporting event. Aside from performing at the Super Bowl, the band also taped a public service announcement that aired during the broadcast. The band members were telling parents how much of an influence they really are in a child's decision whether or not to drink.

In 1999 the band was invited by Pope John Paul II to record a CD of some of his prayers. They also had more than 100 concert dates during 1999. The band attended the Christmas Tree Lighting in New York's Rockefeller Center on December 1, 1999. It was during this surmountable success that the group realized how successful they were and tried to renegotiate their contract with Lou Pearlman and BMG

Records to receive more of the profits from their songs, concerts, and memorabilia.

Pearlman was receiving pay for both managing and producing 'NSync. Of the $10 million the group had earned through albums, concerts, and merchandising, the group allegedly only received three percent of the profits or $300,000. In October 1999, Pearlman sued the group for breach of contract and $150 million. The lawsuit was against both 'NSync and their new record label Jive Records. Backstreet Boys had also left Pearlman to sign with Jive Records. The suit also restricted the band from recording with any other label and using the name 'NSync. The members of 'NSync filed a $25 million countersuit alleging the group was never shown copies of the contract and they were discouraged from involving their lawyers. The court papers describe Pearlman as "a con man . . . who has become wealthy at ('NSync) expense. They have been cheated at every turn by Pearlman's fraud, manipulation, and breach of fiduciary duty."[9] Both the members of the band and their parents were appalled at what they thought Pearlman was doing to them. Chasez, one of the older members of the band, was vocal about the injustices of Pearlman toward the band. Reports claimed that Pearlman was taking about 50 percent of the royalties, 100 percent of advances, and 25 percent of the recording income that the band had made. In a statement Chasez said, "We are painfully aware that our careers may be brief. In truth, our fans made us a success . . . an injunction may be the end of 'NSync. However we cannot work with people who have lied to us."[10] Judge Anne Conway refused to issue an injunction to stop the release of the new 'NSync album with Jive Records. The case was settled and confidentiality agreements had to be signed by all parties.

Pearlman was sued not only by 'NSync, but also by the Backstreet Boys and Aaron Carter. He bought a talent scout agency in September 2002 and proceeded to run a scheme on Internet job search engines. Aspiring stars would answer an ad and then have to use photographers on Pearlman's payroll so he would get a kickback. In 2007 several boy band members and male employees came forward with accusations of sexual misconduct and advances made by Pearlman. His demise came in 2006 when federal investigators started looking into an aviation business that had a lot of investors but existed only in reports. Most of the money invested had been spent by Pearlman. He was arrested in Indonesia in June 2007 and brought back to the United States to await sentencing on mail fraud, bank fraud, and wire fraud. Pearlman received his sentence in 2008 of 25 years in a federal prison for conspiracy, money laundering, and perjury in a bankruptcy hearing. Despite the dishonesty of their first manager, 'NSync went on to sign with a reputable music business, Jive Records.

However, Jive Records has also been criticized by the music industry in their management of 'NSync. Many people believed that the company was focusing mainly on Justin's career instead of the careers of all five band members. Chasez also had good vocal and writing abilities. It is said that the decision of the company to allegedly focus on Justin was why Justin wanted to pursue a solo career.

Although the release of the album was delayed many times due to legal battles, No Strings Attached was released by Jive Records on March 21, 2000. According to Sean Smith in his unauthorized biography, "It sold 2.4 million copies in one week, more than twice the previous record, which was held by their old rivals Backstreet Boys for the album Millennium."[11] No Strings Attached sold 1.13 million copies in only 10 hours. The album featured Diane Warren's "That's When I'll Stop Loving You," and a song produced and arranged by Richard Marx called "This I Promise You." According to Wire magazine, "It sold 1.1 million copies the first day." This made it the fastest selling album of all time.[12] Three singles from the album, "Bye Bye Bye" "It's Gonna Be Me," and "This I Promise You" were in the top five in the United States. During the 76-date tour of the United States, the band made more than $75 million. In March 2000, the band broke Ticketmaster's record for most single-day tickets sold. It became the most popular album of 2000, selling more than 10 million copies. Justin wrote one song on the album titled "I'll Be Good for You." The Recording Industry Association of America confirmed that the album was seven-times platinum; it broke the record set by The Bodyguard soundtrack that reached six-platinum in 1993. The album is the number-one selling 'NSync album worldwide with a total of 11.1 million copies sold. The album also received accolades again in December 2009 by Billboard magazine as being the album of the 2000s decade.

The album cover of No Strings Attached depicted the band members as marionettes without the strings. The message behind the cover was

'NSync was no longer under the control of Pearlman. They had successfully gone out on their own and negotiated a better contract. "By the end of 2000, 'NSync was the world's highest-earning pop music group. They earned more than $267 million in US album sales and tours," according to the book *Justin Timberlake: Breakout Music Superstar*.[13]

In November 2000, 'NSync was sued for $1 million, quickly after the lawsuit with Pearlman was settled. The lawsuit was filed by Sid and Marty Krofft Productions. The production company was responsible for the television shows *H.R. Pufnstuf* and *Land of the Lost*. The company was hired to design puppets of the band members to be used during the performance of "Bye Bye Bye" at the *American Music Awards*. The puppet theme was used on the cover of their *No Strings Attached* album to symbolize the band breaking free from Pearlman. Allegedly, the band used the depictions on posters and other memorabilia without the permission of the Kroffts. The suit was aimed at 'NSync, the individual band members, and the group's manager Johnny Wright. In 2002 Judge Robert Kelleher dismissed all charges against the named defendants. Court documents stated that the Kroffts "cannot establish various liability and no genuine issues remain for trial."[14]

To promote the album, the group set out on tour in the spring of 2000. To be more in tune with the audience the band incorporated sci-fi and vaudeville routines in their performance. The tour garnered more than $70 million for 'NSync and became one of the most successful musical tours of 2000. Many musicians helped the band on their tour including Pink, Lil' Bow Wow, Soul Decision, and Sisqo. MTV aired a special of the tour, which included a backstage look at the concert called *Making the Tour*. The 30-minute special was put into DVD format and included personal time with the band, including dance rehearsals and the band members at home. The concert stop at Madison Square Garden was recorded for an HBO special that later was available on DVD as *'NSync: Live at Madison Square Garden*.

'NSync's album *Celebrity* was released July 24, 2001, by Jive Records. The album is slated as the second-fastest selling album of all time, with the band's first album *No Strings Attached*, being the first. The theme of the album was to reveal the life of a pop star. Several musicians collaborated on the album. In the song "Gone," strings were provided by the Hampton String Quartet. "Up Against the Wall" was written by

Reprock 'n' Alex G. Stevie Wonder played the harmonica on "Something Like You." "Girlfriend" was produced by the Neptunes and Rodney Jenkins, while "Pop" was produced by Brian "BT" Transeau. Almost two million copies of the album were sold in the first week. In an interview with *Teen* magazine, Justin described the group's third album: "I think this album is gonna be even more diverse—a little edgier into the R&B and dance. It's going to be a little bit more mature, but we're still gonna keep the harmonies because that's really our sound."[15]

The PopOdyssey Tour in 2001 was done to promote the *Celebrity* album. The band primarily played venues in North America. The tour boasted pyrotechnics and elaborate stages. Most of the concerts on the tour were sold out. The tour started in Jacksonville, Florida, and featured Lil Romeo and BB Mark. Like their other albums, the band promoted the album with a tour. Sean "P. Diddy" Combs was the opening act. The tour was one the most widely attended concerts of 2001 and boasted earnings of more than $90 million in the United States, even though some concerts had to be cancelled because of Hurricane Season on the Gulf Coast. Because of the success of this tour, 'NSync was forced to add more dates in 2002 and promoted the tour under the *Celebrity* Tour label. This proved profitable for the boy band as they toured North America and earned another $33 million in the United States. A video of the tour came out April 23, 2002, and was titled *PopOdyssey Live*. This would be the last musical tour for 'NSync. On April 28, 2002, in Orlando, the group performed their last concert.

At the 2001 *Video Music Awards*, the band had the chance to be onstage with Michael Jackson, as he demonstrated his dance moves. The Metropolitan Opera House in New York cheered when Jackson was on stage. Being one of Justin's favorite musicians, Justin was disappointed that the band did not perform with Jackson at the *Video Music Awards*. The band was invited to Jackson's 30th anniversary concert, where they did get the opportunity to perform onstage with the music icon. The performance took place at Madison Square Garden in New York. Both 'NSync and Backstreet Boys were slated to perform at Michael Jackson's charity event "United We Stand—What More Can I Give?" in October 2001, to benefit families of the September 11, 2001, tragedy. It was the intention of producers to bring together many popular boy bands and artists. Magid, the producer of the event told *Entertainment Weekly* in an interview, "They ('NSync and Backstreet Boys) were among the first acts that called us. (Backstreet and 'NSync) said, if we can come together as competing entities, if we could put our differences aside, or our rivalry aside, wouldn't this set a great example—and bingo, it's right in front of your eyes."[16] The two boy bands have been on the outs since 'NSync signed with Pearlman. The Backstreet Boys were also with Pearlman and felt as if they were being replaced by 'NSync. The Backstreet Boys left Pearlman to sign with Jive Records. 'NSync followed suit a few years later when they had differences of opinion with Pearlman about money. After 'NSync signed with Jive Records, the Backstreet Boys announced that they were leaving the label.

Many of Michael Jackson's music influences were Justin's musical influences as well, including James Brown and the R&B style of music. Jackson's influence on 'NSync could be seen in their dance moves and the way they tried to captivate an audience with something more than just their lyrics. In an interview with *MTV News* in 2009, after Jackson had passed away, Justin commented, "To create the things that he

'NSync arrives at Michael Jackson's "30th Anniversary Celebration, The Solo Years" concert at New York's Madison Square Garden, September 7, 2001. From left are Lance Bass, Joey Fatone, Justin Timberlake, Chris Kirkpatrick, and JC Chasez. (AP Photo/Tina Fineberg.)

created with his music is untouchable. He opened the minds of the world, to be able to do that through his music . . . (it's) a feat not accomplished by many people, maybe only a handful of people. I don't think anyone ever did it like him."[17]

Although Justin had succeeded in his music career, he had not yet received his high school diploma. Because he joined 'NSync at the age of 14, Justin took a little more time to graduate from high school. For the first year he was in 'NSync, Justin attended school by mail. He then was tutored so he could pursue his singing career. Reveling in all her son's successes, Lynn wanted to make a big deal about Justin receiving his high school diploma. Unbeknownst to Justin, his mother had prepared a ceremony to be held at one of the boy band's performances. While doing a concert in Memphis on May 21, 2000, Justin walked across the stage at an 'NSync concert. When the time came, the band members all got on their hats and gowns and gave one to Justin. Donned in a cap and gown, Justin was given his diploma by Chuck Yerger. The other members of 'NSync wore caps so when Justin got his diploma they could all switch their tassels at the same time.

Justin had been with the group for seven years and was ready to begin a solo career. In an interview with *USA Today*, Justin commented, "I've been doing this thing since I was 12, and 'NSync has been together for seven years. I honestly never expected things to get as big as they did . . . It just got crazy, and I think we all knew we had to take a break, to figure things out."[18] 'NSync's official web site was taken down in 2006.

Justin has no regrets about his seven years with the band. It was rumored that there may be a reunion concert sometime in the future, but the idea was dispelled by Justin in the *Allen Town Morning News* in 2004 when he stated, "I think what we did doesn't work anymore. I think it's kind of hard to make something that was kind of a moment in time, especially when you're all such different people now."[19]

Aside from being a popular boy band that teenagers swooned over, 'NSync also managed to take home many awards during their time. In 2000, they received a nomination at the *Academy of Country Music Awards* for the Top Vocal Event of the Year for the song "God Must Have Spent a Little More Time on You."

From 1999 to 2002 'NSync was nominated for or won an award for every year at the *American Music Awards*. In 1999 the group won Best Pop New Artist. The band was nominated in 2000 for Favorite Band/Duo/Group. For 2001, 'NSync came away with two nominations and an award. Their album, *No Strings Attached*, was nominated for Favorite Pop/Rock Album, and 'NSync was nominated again for Favorite Pop/Rock Band/Duo/Group. To top off the year, the band won Internet Fans Artist of the Year Award. *Celebrity*, the band's third album, was nominated for Favorite Pop/Rock Album at the 2002 awards, while the band itself won Favorite Pop/Rock Band/Duo/Group.

The *Billboard Video Music Awards* in 1998 took place at the MGM Grand Garden Arena in Las Vegas. 'NSync took home two awards and one nomination during the presentation. "I Want You Back" won two of the awards, one for Best Clip (Dance) and the other for Best New Artist Clip. The group was nominated for Best New Artist for "Tearin' Up My Heart."

Between the *Blockbuster Awards* and the *Blockbuster Entertainment Awards*, 'NSync proved very successful. In 1999, the band won the Blockbuster Award for Favorite New Artist/Group. At the 2000 awards, 'NSync's single "Music of My Heart" won Favorite Song from a Movie. The song was from the film of the same name, *Music of My Heart*, written by Diane Warren. The 2001 *Blockbuster Entertainment Awards* garnered 'NSync three wins and one nomination. The band won with Favorite CD, Favorite Pop Group, and Favorite Single for their song "Bye Bye Bye" They received a nomination for Favorite Group overall.

Any band or group's dream is to receive a Grammy nomination or award. During 'NSync's existence, they received eight Grammy nominations but never won a Grammy. In 2000 the group received two nominations for songs that were produced with other artists. With Gloria Estefan, they were nominated for Best Pop Collaboration with Vocals for "Music of My Heart." They also got a nod for Best Country Collaboration with Vocals for "God Must Have Spent a Little More Time on You," with Alabama. Unfortunately, in 2001 'NSync was nominated for three awards but did not win that year. They received a nomination for Best Pop Vocal Album Award for *No Strings Attached*, a Best Pop Performance by a Duo or Group with "Bye Bye Bye," and finally a nomination for Record of the Year for "Bye Bye Bye." In 2002 *Celebrity* was nominated for Best Pop Vocal Album and Best Pop Performance by a Duo or Group for their single "Gone." The group performed at the 2002 *Grammy Awards* with Kevin Federline, Britney's future husband, performing as a dancer. At the 2003 *Grammy Awards,* the band came together to sing a Bee Gees Medley to the Bee Gees. "Girlfriend" was nominated in 2003 for Best Pop Performance by a Duo or Group with Vocals.

At the *Kids Choice Awards* in 2000 and 2001, 'NSync received many nominations but did not win any awards. They were nominated for Favorite Song from a Movie for "Music of My Heart" and a nomination for Favorite Musical Group in 2000. In 2001 they got accolades for Favorite Singing Group and Favorite Song for their hit "Bye Bye Bye."

The *MTV Video Music Awards* garnered the boy bands many awards and nominations. In 1999, however, 'NSync did not win any awards but had four nominations. All four of the nominations were for their hit "Tearin' Up My Heart," for Viewer's Choice, Best Pop Video, Best New Artist Video, and Best Group Video. At the awards in 2000, 'NSync came away with three nominations and two awards for their song "Bye Bye Bye." The song won Best Pop Video and Viewer's Choice and was nominated for Video of the Year, Best Group Video, and Best Dance Video. For their hit single "Pop" the band was awarded with four MTV Video Music Awards and one nomination in 2001. "Pop" won Viewer's Choice, Best Dance Video, Best Pop Video, and Best Group Video. The hit was nominated for Breakthrough Video. In 2002 "Gone" received two nominations at the *MTV Video Music Awards* including Video of the Year and Best Group Video. 'NSync's remix song with Nelly Furtado, "Girlfriend," was nominated for Best Pop Video.

In 2000 the song "Bye Bye Bye" was honored at the *MuchMusic Video Music Awards*. 'NSync won the award for Favorite International Group and the song was nominated for Best International Video. At the *People's Choice Awards* in both 2001 and in 2002, the band won Favorite Musical Group or Band.

As 'NSync's audience is primarily teenagers, it is no wonder that the group took home several Teen Choice Awards between 1999 and 2002. In 1999 their debut album *NSYNC took home the Album of the Year

Award. The song "Bye Bye Bye" won three awards at the 2000 awards including Choice Music Video, Song of the Summer, and Choice Single. That year the band took home the Choice Pop Group. The band won all three of the categories that it was nominated for at the 2001 *Teen Choice Awards*. They won Choice Concert. Their third album, *Celebrity*, won Choice Album, and their song "Pop" won Choice Single. In 2002 their collaboration with Nelly Furtado won Choice Hook Up and was nominated for Choice Single.

The band reconvened in 2005 for the final 'NSync Challenge for the Children but did not perform together. Also in 2005, a greatest hits album was released. The song, "I'll Never Stop" was on the album but had never been released as an American single. Despite the band going their separate ways in 2002, the band was honored with having the best-selling record of the 2000s. Their album, *No Strings Attached*, reached 10 million copies sold for the decade.

In an interview with *Seventeen* magazine, Justin said, "We're brothers. I wouldn't change the friendship I have with them for anything in the world. We like to pick on one another, but it's all in good fun. There's still a level of respect that we have for one another."[20] The band ended as the third best-selling boy band in history.

NOTES

1. Tony Napoli, *Justin Timberlake: Breakout Music Superstar*. Hot Celebrity Biographies. (Berkley Heights, NJ: Enslow Publishers, 2010), p. 18.

2. "Bass: 'I'm Gay and In Love,'" *ContactMusic.com*, July 27, 2006, http://www.sfgate.com/cgi-bin/blogs/dailydish/

3. "Michael Jackson Honored by Justin Timberlake, will.i.am, Diddy," *MTV News*, June 25, 2009, http://www.mtv.com/news/articles/1614756/20090625/jackson_michael.jhtml.

4. Martin Roach, *Justin Timberlake: The Unofficial Book* (London: Virgin Books, 2003), p. 16.

5. Hal Marcovitz, *Justin Timberlake: A View from the Paparazzi* (Broomall, PA: Mason Crest Publishers, 2008), p. 26.

6. "*Precious* Star Reveals 'NSync Obsession," *World Entertainment News Network*, November 15, 2009, http://www.imdb.com/news/ni1194553/.

7. Tom Sinclair, "Grand Ole Opry Teen Pop-ry," *Entertainment Weekly*, September 3, 1999, http://www.ew.com/ew/article/0,,84649,00.html.

8. Roach, *Justin Timberlake*, p. 28.

9. Marcovitz, *Justin Timberlake*, p. 30.

10. Josh Wolk, "'N Rage," *Entertainment Weekly*, November 4, 1999, http://www.ew.com/ew/article/0,,84770,00.html.

11. Sean Smith, *Justin: The Unauthorized Biography* (New York: Pocket Books, 2004), p. 119.

12. Holly Cefrey, *Justin Timberlake: Contemporary Musicians and Their Music* (New York: Rosen Publishing, 2009), p. 23.

13. Napoli, *Justin Timberlake*, p. 24.

14. Josh Grossberg, "'NSync Puppet Case Popped," *E! Online*, April 15, 2002, http://www.eonline.com/uberblog/b43148_sync_puppet_case_popped.html.

15. Marcovitz, *Justin Timberlake*, p. 32.

16. Jocelyn Vena, "Justin Timberlake on Michael Jackson: He 'Was the Baddest'!" *MTV News*, June 30, 3009, http://www.mtvnews.com.

17. Brian Hiatt, "Kings of Pop," *Entertainment Weekly*, October 19, 2001, http://www.ew.com/ew/article/0,,180386,00.html.

18. Steve Dougherty, *Justin Timberlake: Junk Food Tasty Celebrity Bios* (New York: Scholastic, 2009), p. 68.

19. Dougherty, *Justin Timberlake*, p. 93.

20. Laura Morgan, "'NSync Get Down & Dirty," *Seventeen*, July 2001, p. 97.

CHAPTER 4

GOING SOLO

When Justin was still singing with 'NSync he wanted to eventually work on his solo career. He knew he would have to make his first album spectacular to differentiate himself from the boy band. His first solo performance was at the 2002 *MTV Video Music Awards*. The musician sang "Like I Love You." The single was a dance track produced by The Neptunes and was number 11 on the *Billboard* 100. With the release of his first album, Justin felt a new sense of freedom: "I'm going to look back on the summer of 2002 as a time when I created something all on my own. On this album, I'm totally me for the first time in my life. I didn't think about needing a good pop hook—screw it man! I didn't worry about writing a power ballad. It's a new chapter in my life. This is me."[1]

Justin's first performance as a solo artist was August 29, 2002, at the *MTV Video Music Awards*, a couple of months before his first solo album was released. The awards took place at New York City's Radio City Musical Hall. Other artists that participated in the 2002 awards included Eminem and Bruce Springsteen. At the awards, Justin sang "Like I Love You."

Justified, Justin's first solo album, was released on November 5, 2002. It sold more than five million copies. During the first week, 445,000 copies were sold. The sound was more mature and filled with many musicians. It was said to be an album with "legs," meaning "a record people are going buying because they like it and not because they were overtaken by some momentary paroxysm of puppy love."[2]

For "Cry Me a River," Justin wrote the lyrics, and Timbaland and Storch wrote the music. The R&B tune "talks of a relationship soured, a chance lost, a trust destroyed and the irrevocable damage that infidelity causes."[3] The five-minute song is said to be written from Justin's experiences and relationship with Britney Spears. When the video came out for the song there was speculation that it depicted Justin cheating on Spears the way she allegedly cheated on him during their relationship. The woman used in the video bore a striking resemblance to Spears as well. Justin admits he has a "dark side," but he also knows that Spears knows his sense of humor and was probably expecting something like the video. He did phone his former girlfriend to make sure she was alright with the video. In an interview, Justin claimed, "I didn't want things to get misunderstood. She was cool. There's no hard feelings."[4] Despite the controversy surrounding the song, it fared very well with the public. It was this song that sold more than seven million copies of the *Justified* album. The song climbed to number 3 on the *Billboard* charts. He also won a Grammy for Best Male Pop Vocal for "Cry Me a River." The single was also a winner at the *MTV Video Music Awards* with awards for Best Pop Video and Best Male Video. It was nominated for Viewer's Choice and Best Direction at the *MTV Video Music Awards* in 2003. "Rock Your Body," also debuting on the *Justified* album, took Best Dance Video at the 2003 *MTV Video Music Awards*, with "Señorita" being nominated for Best Male Video. Spears also used the breakup to delve into her creativity and write songs. She sang the songs at her Dream with a Dream Concert in Los Angeles.

"Like I Love You," Justin's first solo single released in August 2002, was number 11 on *Billboard* charts. It won a Grammy for Best Rap/Sung Collaboration and was a great way for Justin to add to his credibility as a solo musician. When Justin performed the hit at the MTV awards, critics said he aped Michael Jackson. The song was also produced with the Neptunes.

Justified was a unique album, as it was intended to combine the styles of Justin's favorite musicians including Marvin Gaye, Otis Redding,

Prince, Stevie Wonder, and Michael Jackson. He cowrote 13 songs on the album. "Rock Your Body," number 5 on the *Billboard* charts, included vocals by Vanessa Marquez. "Last Night" was another breakup song included on the album. "(And She Said) Take Me Now," was produced with vocals by Janet Jackson. Vidal Davis and Frank "Knuckles" Walker played percussion on the song "Right for Me." "Señorita" was produced by Pharrell Williams, the Neptunes, and Chad Hugo. Justin and his many musical contributors tried to record most of the music live. Williams and Justin arranged the vocals for every song for the sound engineers. Author Martin Roach wrote, "Much of the album's energy comes from JT's insistence in the studio that they record as many elements as possible live."[5]

What Justin was trying to accomplish with his first solo album was to make something different than what the 'NSync songs were. He wanted something to show that he had matured as a singer and songwriter. With this new direction also came unchartered territory for the singer. He did however work with very skilled musicians who helped him define what the *Justified* album turned out to be. In a *Gentlemen's Quarterly* article, Justin was quoted, "I'll be honest with you because I do not know how else to be. There's not really the push to do the same things. I feel a lack of . . . In some way, shape, or form my inspiration is shifting. When I was putting my album out, I felt the need to see who I was, see what I was all about. And I feel like I've done that. I'll always have that drive. I think that's what makes me who I am. I just don't know specifically where I want to direct it right now."[6]

Williams had worked on five songs for Michael Jackson's *History Volume I* album, but they were rejected by the pop star. The songs then were reworked to be included on Justin's first solo album. The songs included "Señorita," "Let's Take a Ride," "Last Night," "Nothin' Else," and "Take It from Here." Throughout the album, there are certain styles that Justin mimicked from his musical influence Michael Jackson. Many critics compared Justin's first solo album to Michael Jackson's 1979 *Off the Wall* album. There was "a growing resentment in the music business for white men who were trying to sing black music," according to author Sean Smith's book *Justin*.[7]

At the *American Music Awards*, *Justified* won Favorite Pop/Rock Album. Justin himself was nominated at the 2003 *American Music*

Awards for Favorite Pop/Rock Male Artist and was nominated for the Fan Choice Award.

Justin toured a great deal to promote his first solo album. He toured with singer Christina Aguilera and played in the nightclubs and bars in the tour cities. The *Justified* and *Stripped* Tour started out as a 60-city tour but was decreased to 45 cities because tickets were not being sold. The opening night performance in Canada had to be cancelled because equipment trucks were being delayed at the border. The tour included dancers and a band primarily made up of black musicians. The *Justified* Tour opened at Hallam FM Arena in Sheffield. He first used television to promote his album in Britain on *Johnny Vaughn Tonight*. In October 2002, he guest-starred on Britain's *Top of the Pops*, *Radio One*, and *Capital Radio*.

Justin was also interviewed by Barbara Walters on *20/20* the night before his album, *Justified*, was released. Viewers tuned in to see if Justin would reveal anything about his breakup with Spears. However, he had promised Spears he would not speak publicly about their relationship. Justin did entertain viewers by playing "Horrible Woman" on the piano, a single that was not on his upcoming album. ABC executives were using the show to win the ratings for the night. Together with *ABC Monday Night Football*, the network won the night. In 2003, however, the ratings were not as high when NBC aired a music special titled *Justin Timberlake: Down Home in Memphis*. Ironically, ABC's *20/20* beat the NBC special with a Hugh Downs interview with *Playboy* magazine founder Hugh Hefner.

In the United Kingdom the album was rated in the top 10. Justin fell and broke his foot in November 2002 and was forced to cancel promotional concert tours and award presentations on doctor's orders. Justin injured himself while he was rehearsing for the British event, *Smash Hits T4 Poll Winners Party*, which he was to host with singer Kelly Osbourne. His first performance back was at the *Billboard Music Awards* in early December. According to Barry Weiss, president and CEO of Jive Records, Justin, "is hugely important to the industry. In the past three to five years it's become more and more difficult for American artists to sell overseas. He's one of the few that successfully sells in every country around the world."[8]

In the United States, he promoted the album by performing on *All That* and *Saturday Night Live*. He also performed in Times Square in

New York for the MTV television show *Total Request Live*. He sang "Cry Me a River" and "Like I Love You."

It took just six weeks for Justin to write and record *Justified*. Most of his songs and lyrics are based on his personal experiences. After his breakup with Spears, there was a lot of raw emotion that he used to write his songs. He finds writing and recording to be therapeutic: "I sit on my bed, close my eyes, breath deeply and get into a zone. You get that moment where you block everything out, and you just feel, and it takes you to a whole other place. It's kinda like my conversation with God."[9] He cowrote all 13 tracks on the *Justified* album.

Justin's first solo album made critics respect him more as a musician because it combined many different styles. Smith wrote in his biography, "There was a sexuality to the music that the clean-cut image of 'NSync could never allow."[10] The proof of this is the many awards the album received. At the *Brit Awards* in February 2004, the album received Best International Album, and Justin himself received an award for Best International Male Solo Artist. He also performed with Kylie Minogue at the awards. The album was nominated for Album of the Year at the 2004 *Grammy Awards* and won Best Pop Vocal Album of the Year. The song, "Where Is Love?" a collaboration with the Black Eyed Peas, was nominated for Best Rap/Sung Collaboration in 2004 and also nominated for Record of the Year. In 2003, Justin added a collaboration with McDonald's to his resume. He recorded "I'm Lovin' It," to go with McDonald's "I'm Lovin' It" campaign. Justin earned almost $6 million for this project. In September 2003, Justin won a Music of Black Origin (MOBO) award at Royal Albert Hall in London. The awards celebrate various styles of music, including R & B, Jazz, Gospel, and Reggae from artists in England and the United States. Justin was the only male in the category for Best R & B act.

In 2003 Justin was invited to participate in MTV's *New Year's Eve Special*, which was themed a pajama party. Unable to attend, Justin sent his regrets in a video message. His comedic excuse in the video was "he prefers to sleep in the nude and therefore didn't own any PJs to wear for the event."[11] Justin presented an award at the 2003 *Kids' Choice Awards*, but the most outlandish thing he did at the awards was to be crowned the Burping Champ. His belch was loud enough that he did not need a microphone for it to resonate in the crowd. Justin was the host of the MTV *Europe Music Awards* in 2006 that took place in Copenhagen, Denmark. At the awards Justin took home two prestigious awards including Best Male Artist and Best Pop Artist.

On November 16, 2008, Justin joined in the finale for MTV's show *Total Request Live*. The final show was titled *Total Finale Live*. Both Justin and Christina Aguilera shared their memories of when they performed on the show. They were also joined by Beyonce, Taylor Swift, Kid Rock, and fellow 'NSync member JC Chasez. The finale was a big reunion for many musicians who grew up together.

Although Justin's solo albums were four years apart, he found time to enhance his musical career with a variety of collaborations with other musicians. In 2001 he performed with Brian McKnight on his song "My Kind of Girl." Also in 2001, he worked with former girlfriend Spears on her recording of "What It's Like to Be Me." The collaborations continued in 2002 with Nelly on "Work It." He sang with the Black Eyed Peas on their 2003 single "Where Is the Love?" and again in 2005 on their song "My Style" from the album *Monkey Business*. His collaboration with the Clipse on the song "Like I Love You" produced a Grammy nomination in 2003 for Best Rap/Sung Collaboration. After an injured knee caused Spears to postpone her tour, Justin helped her out in 2004 by producing songs with her. Snoop Dogg and Charlie Wilson asked him to sing on the 2005 release "Signs," and in 2005, he recorded with Sergio Mendes, will.i.am, and Pharoahe Monch on "Love Ends" in 2006. He and Nelly worked together again with Timbaland on the single "Give It to Me," which was on Timbaland's 2007 album *Timbaland Presents Shock Value II*. Justin worked with Duran Duran in the summer of 2007. He and Timbaland wrote, produced, and provided vocals for the songs "Nite Runner" and "Falling Down." The two collaborations were on the Duran Duran album *Red Carpet Massacre*, which was released in the United States on November 13, 2007. His work with Duran Duran included helping the group develop a process for their songwriting. In an interview with Reuters, Roger Taylor, Duran Duran's drummer, said, "What they taught us was that you had to be quick and that your first ideas are often the best ideas. We have made quite a few albums which were quite long, tortuous processes."[12] He also presented the award for Best Kiss at the MTV *Movie Awards* to Jake Gyllenhaal and Heath Ledger for the movie *Brokeback Mountain*.

His latest singing projects included T. I.'s hit "Dead and Gone" on T. I.'s *Paper Trail* album. Justin also performed in the music video with T. I. Justin cowrote and produced the single as well as providing the lead vocals. "Dead and Gone" was featured on the iTunes Rewind 2009, its list of best-selling media. The song was honored as number nine on the best-selling songs list. Another song, "If I," was another collaboration from Justin and T. I. and was produced by Timbaland. Justin was in the Nelly Furtado and Timbaland music video, *Promiscuous*, which was released May 3, 2006.

In the spring of 2009, Justin collaborated with Ciara on her song "Love Sex Magic." He also performs with her on the video. The two dance provocatively. Ciara claims she got the idea for the video from something that she saw in a Las Vegas club. Like many artists, Ciara sees the talent and abilities in Justin. She said, "Working with Justin as an artist and producer was really fun for me. He's very cool, very humble. I have a lot of respect for him."[13]

For his second solo album Justin was looking for a fresh new sound so he hired Timbaland and Rick Rubin. The result was *FutureSex/Love-Sounds* which was released September 12, 2006. Producers were amazed at Justin's ability to record and write songs on the spot without writing the lyrics down. The producers on the album included Timbaland, Danja, will.i.am, and Rick Rubin. Justin was influenced by Coldplay, the Killers, and Prince. His first single released from the album, "Sexy-Back," was influenced by the musical styles of David Bowie and David Byrne and was released on July 7, 2006. Several artists provided vocals on the album including Snoop Dogg, Three 6 Mafia, T. I., and will.i.am. Justin used many artists, both of the present and of the past to get a different sound for his songs on his second solo album. According to author Martin Roach, "Just as songs are endlessly covered and remixed, so artists necessarily have to look to the stars of the past in order to create something fresh for the present and the future."[14] In September 2006, *Rolling Stone* magazine referred to Justin as The New King of Pop.

FutureSex/LoveSounds was a hit with two number 1 singles on the charts. The album sold more than 2.4 million copies both in the United States and abroad and was number 1 on the *Billboard* 200 chart. It won the Album of the Year Award. The phrase, "bringing sexy back," was made popular by the single "SexyBack." Timbaland and Nate Hills produced the hit. The single contains the line "Baby, I'm your slave," similar to Spears's song lyrics, "I'm a slave for you." The first single was played more than 85,000 times on MySpace before it had even debuted as a single. The song was number 1 on the *Billboard* 100 chart for seven consecutive weeks. The song garnered a Grammy in 2007 for Best Dance Recording. The video for the hit "What Goes Around . . . / . . . Comes Around" was produced with Samuel Bayer at an estimated cost of more than $1 million. The album was also billed as the biggest album for preorders on the music site iTunes and it also beat Coldplay's previous record of having the largest one-week sales for a digital album. Based on new technology such as YouTube and iTunes, companies are cutting down on costs when it comes to videos. Justin sang the hit song at the 2006 *MTV Video Music Awards* and at the 2006 Victoria Secret Fashion Show. *FutureSex/LoveSounds* was nominated at the 2007 *Grammy Awards* for Album of the Year and Best Pop Vocal Album. The single, "My Love," with T.I., won a Grammy for Best Rap/ Sung Collaboration in 2007. At the *American Music Awards* the album was nominated for Favorite Pop/Rock Album and won the award for Favorite R&B Soul Album. Also that year, Justin won the American Music Award for Favorite Pop/Rock Male Artist.

Justin set out on tour in 2007 to promote the album nationwide. The *FutureSex/LoveShow* tour featured artists such as Pink, Fergie, Natasha Bedingfield, and Esmee Denters, whom Justin signed to the Tennman music label. This was Justin's first solo global tour, with stops in North America, Europe, Asia, and Oceania. According to Reuters, the concert "grossed more than $115.8 million from 100 shows seen by more than 1.5 million people."[15] During his fourth of July concert in London, Justin took a break to honor the troops fighting in Afghanistan and Iraq. To the 18,000-person audience, he exclaimed, "Because it's American Independence Day, I propose a toast. This one goes out to our troops fighting for our freedom."[16] Justin also took a break on the tour at Madison Square Garden to perform his *Saturday Night Live* skit, "Dick in a Box," with Andy Samberg. In Las Vegas and Tacoma, he performed the skit for the crowd solo. For Justin's January 31 birthday concert in Montreal, the crowd serenaded Justin with their rendition of "Happy Birthday." A birthday cake with candles was brought onto the stage and many fans were holding signs that read "Happy Birthday." Timbaland also went on stage to say happy birthday to his fellow producer and also shared a shot of tequila with the singer. The August 16, 2007, concert at Madison Square Concert was recorded by HBO and replayed on the station in September. At the January 11, 2007, concert in San Jose, Justin sang the ballad "(Another Song) All Over Again." He also wore a T-shirt with the saying "You Killed the Part of Me That Cares."

Justin's success was honored throughout 2007 at the many award shows. In the spring of 2007, Justin hosted the *Nickelodeon Kids' Choice Awards* in Los Angeles. In keeping with tradition, he allowed himself to be slimed at the urging of the audience. He and actor Vince Vaughn completed the night by hosing one another with slime and then turning their hoses on the audience. Aside from being the host of the evening, Justin was also an award winner. He took home the Best Male Singer prize. Steve Irwin's (Crocodile Hunter) daughter, Bindi, presented him with the award, which was fitting as Justin gives to Wildlife Warriors Worldwide, a foundation Irwin started before he died. Justin did lose his 2006 coveted award, Celebrity Burp Champion of the World, to the 20,000-people-strong audience.

At the 2007 *Grammy Awards,* Justin performed with Robyn Troup. The Grammy Foundation held a contest, called "My Grammy Moment," with the winner being awarded a performance with Justin during the Grammys. Although Justin was feeling under the weather he did the set anyway. In an interview with *Details* magazine, he stated, "I'm the nice guy who follows through on the things he commits to. But I don't know if I'll be doing that sort of thing again. I feel like the Grammys used me for ratings."[17]

The *Teen Choice Awards* was held at the Gibson Amphitheatre in Universal City, California, on August 27, 2007. Justin was honored with three awards. He won for Male Artist and for his Payback Track "What Goes Around . . . / . . . Comes Around." The most prestigious award he won that night was the Ultimate Choice Award. The award encompassed not only his music but also his achievements. It is the equivalent of a lifetime achievement award that is given out at the Grammys or Emmys. These special awards are not necessarily given out annually.

In 2007 at the *MTV Video Music Awards*, Justin came away with four different awards. He won Male Artist of the Year, Best Director, and Best Choreographer in a video. The fourth award was Quadruple Threat of the Year. His song "What Goes Around . . . / . . . Comes Around" was nominated for Video of the Year and Best Editing, while his collaboration with Timbaland on "SexyBack" was nominated for Most Earth-Shattering Collaboration. The proof of his success as a solo artist came in 2007 when he was billed as the "World's Best Selling Pop Male Artist of the Year" and the "World's Best Selling American Artist of the Year." On the *Billboard* charts' Top Artists of 2007, Justin was labeled number three, while R&B singer Akon took the top spot.

In 2008 Justin was awarded two Grammys for songs on his second album. He won the Male Pop Performance Award for "What Goes Around . . . / . . . Comes Around." For "Love Stoned/I Think She Knows," he was given the Dance Recording Award. Also, in 2008 "What Goes Around . . . / . . . Comes Around" was nominated for Record of the Year. "Give It to Me," a song with Timbaland and Nelly Furtado, was given a Grammy nomination for Best Pop Collaboration with Vocals. The song, "Ayo Technology," with 50 Cent and Timbaland, was nominated in 2008 for Best Rap Song.

On September 18, 2007, MCA Nashville released *Reba Duets*, a collaboration with many artists including Justin, Kenny Chesney, Don Henley, and Kelly Clarkson. Reba chose to do a duet album because it was her last project with the MCA label and she wanted to do something extraordinary. With all the artists having different schedules and being in other locations, a duet album was a huge undertaking. Reba enjoyed working with Justin because he was so versatile and accommodating. Justin cowrote the song he sang with Reba called "The Only Promise That Remains."

In spring 2008, Justin found himself recording with Madonna on her song "4 Minutes," which was on Madonna's 11th album, *Hard Candy*. When they began recording, Justin and Madonna were gun-shy around each other never having worked together before. However, Madonna immediately felt comfortable around him and recognized his talent. In an interview, she commented, "He's ambitious but not in an offensive way. He's incredibly responsible and he's good at what he does and I think he has a long future in front of him. He understands the insanity of being a pop star."[18] Justin performed at Madonna's *Hard Candy Promo Show* in New York City and on November 6, 2008, at Madonna's Sticky & Sweet Tour, at Los Angeles' Dodger Stadium. The two performed "4 Minutes." Spears, Justin's former girlfriend, also surprised concert goers, but the two musicians did not perform together. The song was nominated for Favorite Combined Forces at the *People's Choice Awards*, but the pair lost to Jordin Sparks and Chris Brown for their song "No Air." The song was also nominated for two Grammys in 2009, including Best Pop Collaboration with Vocals and Best Remixed Recording. Justin believes that Madonna is a great artist, and the two collaborated on more than five songs when they were in the studio. Justin characterized Madonna as a workaholic: "Her ethic is kinda infectious in the studio. I was like, 'I'm too slow, I'm too slow.' She's a workhorse and I'm just a fan . . . who tricked Madonna."[19] Earlier in March, Justin introduced Madonna as she was inducted into the Rock and Roll Hall of Fame. In his introduction, he told a story about the two of them in the recording studio. He recalled that he was not feeling well on one occasion and Madonna proceeded to help by giving him a vitamin B_{12} injection in his rear end. The two squabbled about the accuracy of the wording of what was said during the incident. Madonna claimed she politely said, "Pull your pants down," while Justin recalls her matter-of-factly stating, "Drop 'em." When Madonna complimented Justin on his "top shelf," he thought it was the greatest day of his life.[20] The event took place March 10, 2008, at the Waldorf-Astoria Hotel in Manhattan. Justin had had previous experience with the induction ceremony, when in 2005 he inducted the R&B vocal band the O'Jays into the Hall of Fame.

Justin also collaborated with Madonna on the video *4 Minutes to Save the World*. It was directed by Jonas Francois, who also worked with Justice, Maroon 5, and James Blunt. Filmed in London, the video was released with Madonna's *Hard Candy* album in January 2008. During the recording on his 27th birthday, January 31, Madonna presented Justin with a cupcake and champagne and sang "Happy Birthday" to her colleague. He also participated in *In Style* magazine's "Grammy Salute to Fashion." The first-annual event, on February 7, 2008, showcased fashion collections from Justin, Beyonce, Jay-Z, Jessica Simpson, Jennifer Lopez, and others.

Madonna, left, is joined by Justin Timberlake for a duet during her performance to celebrate the release of her new CD Hard Candy *at Roseland Ballroom, April 30, 2008, in New York. (AP Photo/Evan Agostini.)*

In late 2008, Justin recorded two new songs, titled "Steppin' Out Tonight" and "Magic." Rihanna's video from her single, "Rehab," was released in late 2008. It featured Justin as her love interest. The song is from Rihanna's album *Good Girl Gone Bad*. Justin, along with Timbaland and Hannon Lane, wrote the song. Justin also provided vocals for the song. In 2009 Justin also worked with Rihanna on her *Rated R* album on the song "Cold Case Love," a song that Justin had written. Justin was also supportive of Rihanna when she and Chris Brown had their domestic dispute in early 2009. Late in 2008, Justin worked with T-Pain on his song "Can't Believe It." Originally, Lil Wayne was on the remix, but he was replaced by Justin. T-Pain was elated that Justin would pick his song to do his first remix: "It's just awesome when someone who don't ever do remixes with anyone hopped on my song out of every hot record out there. I never expected it to happen."[21] By the end of 2008, Justin was declared among one of the best paid singers in the world in 2008.[22]

Justin attended the *Grammy Awards* in the beginning of 2009 where he was nominated for two awards with Madonna for their collaboration on "4 Minutes." Although the song did not win any awards, Justin was happy for the others that did win. Adele, a British soul singer, won the award for Best New Artist and Best Female Pop Vocal Performance. At the end of the presentations, Justin had tried to congratulate the newcomer on her award, but because of the commotion did not receive a heartfelt response. Adele felt badly about the encounter and apologized: "Justin, I love you and I'm really sorry . . . for making it seem like I didn't want to meet you. I really did—and I don't think we can ever be friends because you're just too much. You're too good."[23]

Justin was supposed to perform with Rihanna at the 2009 *Grammy Awards*, but at the last minute, Rihanna backed out of even attending the Grammys due to her altercation with then-boyfriend Chris Brown. When Justin arrived in his dressing room, there were several executives there to tell Justin that there was a problem with the lineup of the show. In an improvisational moment, Justin suggested he sing with gospel singer Al Green. Green, Justin, Boys II Men, and Keith Urban sang "Let's Stay Together."

In the spring of 2009, Justin had no plans to produce and release another solo album. He continues to build his solo career in collaborating with other musicians. To do another album, Justin believes he would have to reserve at least two years of his life to write and record it. "Committing to my own sort of project, that's like, 'Okay, let me block out two years of my life and do it.' I was heavily fulfilled with the last one and I always have this thing with myself that if I can't sleep because I need to do it, then I'm gonna do it. But if I am not losing sleep over it then . . .," he said in an interview with *Entertainment Weekly*.[24]

In the summer of 2009, Justin helped produce and sang vocals on Leona Lewis's album *Echo*, released November 17, 2009, in the United States. He wrote and provided vocals on the song "Don't Let Me Down." The track was produced at Chalice Recording Studio with Justin's personal production team, The Y's. Before the collaboration, Lewis was nervous about working with such a celebrity musician. In an interview with the *Daily Star*, she commented, "He is a beautiful boy and I was a bit worried whether it would cloud my judgment over whether the song was good or not. But as soon as I met him that was over."[25] She believes they are both focused people. Together with Pharrell Williams, Justin remixed songs from the band Kings of Leon. Justin worked with The Game on his *R.E.D. Album* in late 2009. Also in 2009, Justin performed with producer Timbaland on his album *Shock Value II,* on the song "Carry Out." Justin debuted the single at his benefit concert in November. The video was released in 2010.

At the end of 2009, many web sites were citing Justin as one of the most influential musicians of the decade. Hitfix named him one of the top trendsetters of the decade. On the British web site Popstar.com, Justin's second solo album, *FutureSex/LoveSounds* earned the honor of being named album of the decade. The celebrity news site *AceShowBiz* billed Ciara and Justin's video for "Love Sex Magic" as one of the Ten Most Outrageous Videos of the Year. Videos are chosen on the basis of their shocking content and for ability to raise controversy. The song, "Love Sex Magic", was also nominated for a Grammy for Best Pop Collaboration.

With all the collaborations that Justin has done in his solo career, he is appealing to diverse audiences. He is constantly making things better and recording with different people in the studio to make different sounds. He put his solo career on hold to make time to collaborate with a variety of musicians. In an interview at his 2008 charity concert for the Shriners Hospital, Justin told *MTV News,* "As far as myself, I don't have that . . . I could change next week, but I don't have the bug to jump in and start the whole process again, and touring again, I do love it, but it's tiring."[26] This is what makes him a successful performer, the ability to transform his music into different styles to appeal to various audiences. According to author Sean Smith, "Justin will always have a following of prepubescent girls, but longevity in the music business requires an audience with more financial muscle than the girls' pocket money. It usually also requires continual rejuvenation."[27]

One of the biggest influences in Justin's music and style was Michael Jackson. He mimicked his hats, skinny ties, and black pants with white socks. Justin emulated Jackson's singing and the way he had influenced generations of people. In an interview with *MTV News,* Justin commented, "Growing up in Tennessee, I never really understood the phenomenon that was Michael Jackson or the pandemonium that followed him around. I just heard certain songs that I loved as a kid and I gravitated toward those songs. It just so happens that 99.97 percent of his songs are perfect. They're perfect songs. The other whatever percent are works of art as well."[28] Many have criticized Justin for trying to be like Michael Jackson in his dance moves and hip-hop style.

Producer Timbaland had compared teen singing sensation Miley Cyrus to Justin. The producer has worked with both of these artists and sees the similarities between their work ethic and their music. The two musicians have started out in the music business at a very young age. Both come from musical Southern backgrounds and have developed a love for singing that was to some degree developed in church. They have both worked for the Disney Corporation. The success that these two stars have achieved has also come from the support that they have received from their family members. Justin and Cyrus have been seen in newspaper and magazine articles with their family members in tow backing them up. In an interview with *E! Online,* Timbaland said, "Man, she's gonna be like Justin Timberlake. She comes from that same musical background, where she's just got it."[29] When the media were brandishing Cyrus about her so-called scandalous pictures in *Vanity Fair* magazine and the images that appeared on the Internet, Justin came to her defense. He attributed the fanfare to the era of technology and the willingness to find fault with a celebrity. "Of course they're going to pick on a wholesome, American, young female for the first sign of anything. Unfortunately, there's a picture with her just in a blanket. . . . And that's THE photo, that's the catalyst. But that's also the age we live in. People want to take a photo, and that's who you are for a year's time. We've all become victims of that," he said in an interview.[30] Justin knows first-hand the effects technology can have on a scandal based on his controversy with the 2004 Super Bowl. His wardrobe malfunction was constantly in the media.

Like other musicians and celebrities, Justin knows he would be nowhere without his fans. Although he values his privacy and does not like to be followed, he realizes as a celebrity there comes with it the stress of being watched and criticized. He becomes very humble when it comes to his fan base: "The fans have been great to me. I don't think it's asking too much to have me sign something for them."[31]

NOTES

1. Laura Morgan, "Just 'NSide," *Seventeen*, November 2002, p. 137.

2. Devin Friedman, "Icon," *Gentlemen's Quarterly*, September 2004, p. 356.

3. Martin Roach, *Justin Timberlake: The Unofficial Book* (London: Virgin Books, 2003), p. 47.

4. "Britney 'Cool' about Justin's Video," *World Entertainment News Network*, January 8, 2003, http://wenn.com.

5. Roach, *Justin Timberlake*, p. 49.

6. Friedman, "Icon," p. 359.

7. Sean Smith, *Justin: The Unauthorized Biography* (New York: Pocket Books, 2004), p. 182.

8. Clark Collis, "Sexy Beat," *Entertainment Weekly*, February 9, 2007, p. 35.

9. Austin Scaggs, "Justin Timberlake Revs Up His Sex Machine," *Rolling Stone Magazine*, September 21, 2006, p. 50.

10. Smith, *Justin*, p. 178.

11. Jocelyn Vena, "Miley Cyrus, Justin Timberlake More Ring in the New Year with MTV: A Look Back," *MTV News*, December 30, 2009, http://www.mtvnews.com.

12. Michelle Nichols, "Timberlake Helping Duran Duran Get Sexy Back," Reuters, November 3, 2007, http://www.reuters.com/article/idUSN0252228420071105.

13. Jocelyn Vena, "Ciara Heats Up with Justin Timberlake in 'Love Sex Magic,'" *MTV News*, March 23, 2009, http://www.mtvnews.com.

14. Roach, *Justin Timberlake*, p. 57.

15. Michelle Nichols, "The Police Win Billboard Top Tour," Reuters, November 15, 2007, http://www.reuters.com/article/idUSN15333 71820071117.

16. Drew Tewksbury, "Justin Timberlake's Patriotic Shout-Out," *People*, July 5, 2007, http://www.people.com.

17. "Timberlake Regrets Grammy Awards Talent Showcase," *World Entertainment News Network*, March 22, 2007, http://wenn.com.

18. Jackie Fields, "Madonna and Justin Timberlake 'Tie One On' After Concert," *People*, May 1, 2008, http://www.people.com

19. "Madonna Invites Timberlake Back to the Studio," *World Entertainment News Network*, May 8, 2007, http://wenn.com.

20. Chris Harris, "Madonna Shocks, Justin Timberlake Pays Tribute at Rock and Roll Hall of Fame Ceremony," *MTV News*, March 11, 2008, http://www.mtvnews.com.

21. "Madonna Invites Timberlake Back to the Studio."

22. Shaheem Reid, "Justin Timberlake Jumps on T-Pain's 'Can't Believe It' Remix," *MTV News*, November 10, 2008, http://www.mtv news.com.

23. Jocelyn Vena, "Adele Apologizes for Snubbing Justin Timberlake at Grammys," *MTV News*, March 5, 2009, http://www.mtvnews.com.

24. Tim Stack, "Justin Timberlake Exclusive: The Singer on His New Album (or Lack Thereof) and Current iPod Favorites," *Entertainment Weekly*, March 25, 2009, http://www.ew.com.

25. "Leona 'Was Nervous Meeting Timberlake,'" *Digital Spy*, November 12, 2009, http://www.digitalspy.com.

26. Jocelyn Vena, "Justin Timberlake Retires 'SexyBack,' Rocks with 50 Cent at Las Vegas Concert," *MTV News*, October 20, 2008, http://www.mtvnews.com.

27. Smith, *Justin*, p. 160.

28. Eric Ditzian, "Justin Timberlake on Michael Jackson: '99.97 Percent of His Songs Are Perfect,'" *MTV News*, October 20, 2009, http://www.mtvnews.com.

29. Tim Stack, "Timbaland on Miley Cyrus: She's the Next Justin Timberlake," *Entertainment Weekly*, November 12, 2009, http://www.ew.com.

30. James Montgomery with John Norris, "Justin Timberlake Thinks Miley Cyrus a Victim of 'The Age We Live In,'" *MTV News*, May 5, 2008, http://www.mtvnews.com.

31. James DeMedeiros, *Justin Timberlake: Remarkable People Series* (New York: Weigl Publishers, 2009), p. 11.

CHAPTER 5

THE ACTOR

Like many musicians, Justin tried his hand at acting on both television and in films. He had already had acting experience from when he did comedy sketches on *The All-New Mickey Mouse Club*. In an interview with *Rolling Stone*, Justin commented that he needed something different to motivate him: "The reason I got into film is because I needed something inspiring, but more intimate, that I didn't have to do in front of 18,000 people every night."[1]

Disney also gave Justin his first film job in the Disney Channel television movie *Model Behavior*. Debuting on March 12, 2000, the show is based on the book *Janine and Alex, Alex and Janine*, by Michael Levin. The movie was filmed in Toronto and directed by Mark Rosman. Other stars in the film include Kathie Lee Gifford, Maggie Lawson, Jesse Nilson, and Cody Gifford. The movie is about two teenage girls who switch places to have totally different experiences. Justin plays the role of Jason Sharp, a young, handsome model who dates one of the teenagers that switched places. He is using the teenage model to further his own career.

In 2003 he became known as "the man Ashton Kutcher almost made cry."[2] He was the first victim on Ashton Kutcher's new show

Punk'd. The show is similar to *Candid Camera* or *TV's Bloopers and Practical Jokes*. Kutcher chooses a celebrity to lay a prank on and airs it on national television. Actors posing as IRS agents went to Justin's home to take his possessions because of nonpayment of back taxes. Justin's prank was in the first episode of the first season. It is listed as one of Kutcher's top-ten *Punk'd* episodes. Kutcher has punked other musicians that Justin has worked with through the years including Pete Wentz, Kanye West, and Beyonce Knowles. Justin retaliated by doing a skit about Kutcher when he hosted and was the musical guest on *Saturday Night Live (SNL)* in October 2003. He appeared again on *Punk'd* to help Kutcher set up Kelly Osbourne. In the show with Osbourne, Justin was Ashton Kutcher's stand in. Justin became the only celebrity to appear on the television show more than once.

He was invited back several times to host *SNL*. Justin referred to the *SNL* set as "a playground."[3] His skit with Andy Samberg called "Dick in a Box" became a popular comedy sketch. The skit ran unedited on YouTube and had just as many viewers as the *SNL* show did. The video started with a warning about language and content not being suitable for all viewers. Rick Ludwin, head of late-night programming on NBC, was skeptical about the skit being shown on YouTube because it still represented NBC, but it became one of the most-watched videos. Justin helped compose the R&B music that went with the skit. It was a video about gift-wrapped manhoods. Justin won a Creative Emmy for his "Dick in a Box" skit. He won for Best Original Music and Lyrics. Actor Forest Whitaker sang a classical arrangement of the skit at the 2009 *MTV Movie Awards*. *Incredibad*, an album with all the vocals from the SNL skits, debuted in early 2009. The album included "Dick in a Box," "Lazy Sunday," and "Natalie Raps." Aside from Justin, other musical collaborators included T-Pain, Jack Black, and The Strokes singer Julian Casablancas. Along with Jimmy Fallon, Justin also did a spoof of the Bee Gees on *SNL*. He and Samberg worked on another skit for *SNL* titled "Motherlover," in honor of Mother's Day. It was a ballad about the two characters having relations with each other's widowed mothers. The two mothers were played by Susan Sarandon and Patricia Clarkson. The two musicians, Justin and Samberg, wrote the lyrics together. In 2009 the skit was nominated for an Emmy for Outstanding Original Music and Lyrics. In November 2008, Justin made another guest appearance on *SNL*. Wearing a one-piece swimming suit and high heels, he was one of Beyonce Knowles backup dancers in the song "Single Ladies (Put a Ring on It)." Justin was hosting *SNL* for the third time when Ciara was the musical guest. He tried to put the songstress at ease by telling jokes before the two went on stage to perform "Love Sex Magic" from her album *Fantasy Ride*. The parodied music video was directed by Seth Myers. *SNL* aired a Christmas special in 2009 called *A Very Gilly Christmas*. The episode featured clips from when Justin was the host as well as his controversial comedy skits with Andy Samberg. In 2009 Justin was also the first guest on Jimmy Fallon's late night show when he took over for Conan O'Brien. Fallon took over the late show on March 2, 2009. The former *SNL* cast member and Justin did a skit on *SNL* called *The Barry Gibbs Talk Show*.

In 2009 he received an Emmy Award for his work on *SNL*. Justin made history by being the first *SNL* host to win an Emmy. Out of 22 hosts, Justin won for Best Actor in a Comedy Series. The actors he was up against for the award included television veteran Alan Alda, for his work in *30 Rock*. Beau Bridges was nominated for his guest-starring role in the 100th episode of *Desperate Housewives*. Other nominees included Steve Martin and Jon Hamm. Justin was the second youngest actor to achieve the award beside Bobby Cannavale who received the Emmy for his reoccurring role on *Will & Grace*. Because of his comedic timing and natural acting ability, he received many acting offers. Justin won a Creative Arts Emmy for hosting *SNL* in 2009. Justin hosted the *MTV Movie Awards* in 2003 with *American Pie* actor Seann William Scott. The dynamic pairing of these two hosts celebrated the year in movies.

After the Super Bowl incident in 2004, Justin was ready to take a break with music and concentrate his efforts on something else. In the summer of 2004, Justin acted in the movie *Edison Force*. The film was released July 18, 2006 in the United States and was a straight-to-video film. After being played at several film festivals, the movie received many bad reviews. He appeared with Morgan Freeman and Kevin Spacey. Justin was billed third behind the two stars. It was filmed in Vancouver, Canada. Justin plays Josh Pollack, a young journalist who uncovers corruption in the police department. He enlists the help of his editor and another veteran reporter to help him. Although the film was not in theaters, it was presented at the Toronto Film Festival.

The next foray into film was more successful in the drama *Alpha Dog*. Directed by Nick Cassavetes, this movie was based on an actual Los Angeles murder and the life of California gangster Jesse James Hollywood. A 15-year-old boy, Nicholas Markovitz, was kidnapped and murdered for a drug debt his older brother had. Hollywood is awaiting charges and, if convicted, could be sentenced to the death penalty. In October 2006, Hollywood sued Universal Studios and wanted an injunction to stop the film from being released. The film depicts the kidnapping and murder of Zack Mazursky in a shallow grave in the Hollywood Hills. Justin played one of the kidnappers, Frankie Ballenbacher. He and other gangsters take Zack to the grave at the request of their leader Johnny Truelove, who runs drugs for a living. He believes the only way to stop Zack from talking about their operation is to murder him. In the film, Frankie gets a life sentence in prison when he is caught. Johnny Truelove escapes to Paraguay and would not be found until five years later but is on the FBI's Most Wanted List. It had already been shown at the Sundance Film Festival. Hollywood believed the film would not let him receive a fair trial because it was allegedly based on the former prosecutor's events of the case. Director Cassavetes based his film on the numerous documents he could get his hands on including prosecution notes, public records, and the Markovitz family's details of what happened. The character that Justin plays has already been convicted and is serving a life sentence for the crime. In reality Jesse James Hollywood was convicted of first-degree murder and kidnapping and was sentenced to life in prison. To prepare for his role, Justin and Cassavetes took a trip to the jail for character development. In an interview with *MTV News*, Justin commented, "It was nice to get his perspective, get a feel for the guy, to make sense of this nonsensical travesty. But what's he going to say? He's serving a life sentence. He is pretty unhappy."[4] Along with Emile Hersch and Bruce Willis, Justin was known as a tattooed gangster. He wanted a dramatic, controversial role, and this was going to be Justin's mark on the film world. "I thought it was a dark script, but I also thought that it was a great statement and I like to make statements," Justin commented.[5] Although producers wanted Justin to take acting classes for the role, critics were positive about Justin's acting abilities in *Alpha Dog*. He was nominated for an MTV Movie Award in 2007 for his performance. He also received a nomination for a Teen Choice Award for Breakout Male Performance in *Alpha Dog*.

For the premiere of the movie *Alpha Dog*, Justin brought his mother, Lynn. Justin enjoys being with his mother and did not mind sharing his time with her at the afterparty at Ivar Studios. It wasn't until almost midnight that the pair went on to the club Social Hollywood. Justin, Scarlett Johansson, and Lynn danced until the bar closed at 2 A.M. Also at the bar were other actors and actresses from the film including Emile Hirsch, Shawn Hatosy, Ben Foster, and Olivia Wilde. Justin had said in interviews previously that he enjoys going out on the town with his mother and that frequently she stays out later than he does.

With rave reviews, Justin continued his film career with *Southland Tales* as Private Pilot Abilene. It is a thriller about a terrorist attack on the United States. The narrator of the film is a disfigured veteran of the Iraq War. The story line begins in Abilene, Texas, after a nuclear weapon is set off during July 4, 2005, festivities. The two nuclear weapons unleashed on Texas caused the nation to go into turmoil and produced a World War III between Iraq, Afghanistan, Syria, and Korea. Because of the attacks, Texas is now facing an energy and oil crisis. Several government agencies try to rectify the situation. They are being opposed by extremist and rebellious groups that must be stopped. The film is dubbed as an apocalyptic view of the end of the world in which the end of the world does not occur. The film debuted at the Cannes Film Festival to mixed reviews as audiences were looking for different endings to the movie. The film was revamped after the festival to include more special effects, clarification of the narrator's points of view, and an ending change.

Shortly following *Southland Tales* was another drama, *Black Snake Moan*. Justin played Ronnie, the boyfriend of Rae, played by Christina Ricci. An aging bluesman, played by Samuel L. Jackson, helps Rae get back on her feet after her parents both physically and verbally abuse her. Lazarus himself is dealing with the issue of his wife leaving him. Ronnie misinterprets the relationship between Rae and the bluesman Lazarus after he is discharged from the service due to anxiety issues. Ronnie's friend Gill, played by Michael Raymond-James, is helping Ronnie and is putting ideas in his head about Rae and Lazarus. He vows to kill Lazarus to win back the full affections of his girlfriend.

In the end, Lazarus helps Ronnie understand that he is only helping Rae and in turn also helps Ronnie with his issues. The film debuted at the Sundance Film Festival.

Ricci, Justin's costar in the film, was impressed by Justin's acting abilities. Ricci and Justin had a couple of intimate scenes that were a bit awkward, but Ricci and Justin felt comfortable with each other and laughed about the scenes afterward. Ricci was wowed by Justin's ability to easily transform himself into the character of an Iraq veteran. "It's not a vanity project. And he's not in a place where he needs to prove himself. He's established in his market, so he doesn't have to be choosing to do roles like this. It really shows the true inklings of an artist," Ricci commented.[6]

Apart from acting in films, he also provided his voice to *Shrek the Third* in 2007 as Prince Artie Pendragon. Together with Eddie Murphy, Mike Meyers, and Cameron Diaz, Justin fit in comedically into the film. Speculation was that Justin received the voice-over part because of his relationship with then-girlfriend Diaz. Aron Warner, the producer of *Shrek the Third,* quashed the rumors stating, "Our desire was to get somebody who is visible and had their own persona to bring to the table. Justin fit the bill perfectly."[7] Justin had already been seen in *Shrek 2*. A picture of Sir Justin was pictured on the wall in Princess Fiona's bedroom. The role of Artie was reprised in the 2010 release of *Shrek Forever After.*

Yogi Bear, released in 2010, includes Justin as Boo-Boo, Yogi's sidekick. Yogi is played by Dan Aykroyd. A filmmaker, Rachel, played by Anna Faris, comes to check out Jelly Stone Park to possibly film a documentary there. The Mayor, voiced by Andy Daly, has used all the money for the city and wants to sell Jelly Stone Park to pay back debts. Yogi and Boo-Boo Bear join forces with their enemy, Ranger Smith, animated by Tom Cavanagh. The ranger and the filmmaker become romantically involved through the exploits of Yogi and Boo-Boo. Donald DeLine produced the film. In 2009 he also lent his voice to the animated television show *Family Guy.*

In the spring of 2008, Justin was approached by NBC to be the executive producer of a new comedy show called *My Problem with Women.* The show was an adaptation of a Peruvian comedy, titled *Mi Problema con las Mujeres.* It is a story about Jose, a man in his thirties who begins to see a therapist to find out why all his relationships fail. NBC had success in the past adapting foreign shows such as *The Office* and *Ugly Betty*.

In 2008 Justin costarred in *The Love Guru* with Mike Myers. He plays Jacques Grande, a Kings hockey player who stole the affections of his rival Darren Roanoke's wife. Pitka, the guru, has been hired by the Toronto Maple Leafs to help their player get out of his funk and win back the affections of his wife. The film was produced in Toronto, Canada, and also included Jessica Alba, Meagan Good, and Ben Kingsley. Jessica Simpson, Kanye West, and Deepak Chopra made cameos as themselves in the film. Despite the well-known singers and celebrities in the film, the movie topped the Worst Movie List of 2008 put out by the *New York Post*. The newspaper claimed the film was "unfunny and embarrassing."[8] Also in the top of the list were *The Hottie and the Nottie*, *Mad Money*, and *What Happens in Vegas*. Justin appeared in the trailer for the movie in a Speedo, a moustache, and a French accent.

In Elton John's video for the song "The Train Don't Stop There Anymore," Justin portrayed the young Elton John. The made-for TV movie *Elton John: The Red Piano* is a commentary about his three-decade career. It features his Las Vegas club act, as well as an appearance by Pam Anderson, dancing on a pole. Justin also portrays the young Elton John in the song "Rocket Man." Elton John made the comment in the *London Daily Sun* in regard to Justin's performance: "He's a really talented boy, he gave me the chills when I watched him in the video. It was actually so close to me."[9]

Released August 28, 2009, *The Open Road* was a movie about the son of a baseball star who goes on a road trip to find his father when his mother gets sick. The premise of the plot line is that it is more about the journey than about the destination as the father and son travel back to his mother's bedside. Justin plays the son, Carlton Garrett, while Jeff Bridges plays the father, Kyle. Mary Steenburgen plays the mother. Justin's character as a baseball player feels lost in his legendary baseball player father's shadow and uses the road as a way to determine what is really important in life. Some of the scenes were shot in Whataburger Field in Corpus Christi, Texas, while some scenes were shot in Hammond, Louisiana.[10] The film was written and directed by Michael Meredith, whose father is legendary Cowboys football player

"Dandy Don" Meredith. For the movie Justin tried to get in touch with real baseball stars in Texas but schedules for the team and Justin did not coincide. Despite the well-known cast, *The Open Road* did not fare too well in theaters, making only $13,000 among 14 theaters in its first weekend.

Stepping into the director's mode in April 2009, Justin directed and produced the MTV reality series *The Phone*. The show is based on a Dutch television show of the same name. The premise of the show is that four real-life individuals, not actors, are put in dangerous physical and mental situations. Each contestant has a chance to win $50,000 each episode. The series consists of six, one-hour-long episodes. The players answer a phone call which then throws them into a plot to win the money. They are asked by the Operator if they would like to participate in the game. If they answer affirmatively, they are in constant contact with the Operator who gives them tasks throughout the show. Unfortunately, in its debut episode, the show only attracted 920,000 viewers. There have been six missions, "The Bomber," "The Conspiracy," "The Wise Guys," "The Russians," "The Triad," and "The Drug Cartel." In an interview with *MTV News*, Justin described the show: "Just like a thriller or suspense film at the end of the show, every show, there is a twist that we put on the contestants."[11]

With the increasing demand for Internet network sites, Michael DeLuca Productions filmed *The Social Network* in 2010. Columbia Pictures distributed the film and was rumored to have budgeted almost $47 million for the film. Justin plays Sean Parker, cofounder of Napster and Facebook's president, along with Jesse Eisenberg as Mark Zuckerberg, the founder of the popular social site Facebook. Justin's character is a party-by-night and wheel-and-deal-by-day kind of man. For the movie, Justin also goes back to sporting his curly hair like he did back in the day when he was in the band 'NSync. Zuckerberg founded Facebook at the age of 19 with some of his roommates while he was at Harvard. The film is based on the book *Accidental Billionaires: The Founding of Facebook A Tale of Sex, Money, Genius and Betrayal* by Ben Mezrich. Aaron Sorkin, who wrote the script, has a knack for creating drama and suspense out of reality. His film credits also include *Charlie Wilson's War* and *The Trial of the Chicago 7*. His television credits include *The West Wing*, *Studio 60 on the Sunset Strip*, and *Sports Night*. It was directed by

David Fincher who also directed *The Curious Case of Benjamin Button* and *Panic Room*. The film deals with two people who got rich too fast and the obstacles the two had to overcome. It has all the elements of a dramatic tale including wealth and betrayal. Although the film takes place in Boston, Justin filmed his scenes in California. The movie was approved for up to $5 million in tax credits from the state of California under the film incentive plan. In 2009 the film made Hollywood executives Black List, movies they think will be great in the next year but have not yet finished production. "Launched in 2004, Facebook has emerged as the world's leading social networking site, with more than 300 million users," according to the *Los Angeles Times*.[12]

Aside from films, Justin has also appeared on popular television shows during the 2000s. Besides his work on *SNL*, he has also appeared on *Sabrina the Teenage Witch*, *Sesame Street*, *Clueless*, *MADTV*, and *Touched by an Angel*. In a 2003 episode of *Will & Grace*, Justin plays a gay gentleman gigolo who wins the affections of Jack, played by Sean Hayes. He signed a three-episode contract for shows during the series' eighth and final season. He donated his $50,000 paycheck from the episode to the AIDS organization. Also in 2003, he was in talks to be a correspondent for TNT and TBS sports telecasts. According to reports in the *New York Post*, Justin considered himself just a fan of basketball. Michael Pearl, producer and executive of Turner Sports, commented, "The key is that he (Justin) doesn't want—and was very firm in this—he doesn't want to pretend to be a sports expert. Because he's not. He's just a very big sports fan."[13] Justin found one of his assignments to be an interview with Magic Johnson. He interviewed the player and had time to play hoops with him in a segment titled *NBA Playoffs . . . Justified*. Aside from being a sports correspondent, Justin also appeared on *Inside the NBA* with Michael Jordan. In 2002 and 2003, he participated in the NBA All-Star Weekend and played against Johnson in TNT's *989 Sports All-Star Hoop It Up* in February 2002. He also participated in the NBA promotional campaign "Can't Get Enough."

He has hosted many award shows, including the *ESPN Espy Awards* in 2008 and the 2007 *Kids' Choice Awards* in New York, and he also introduced Madonna at the Rock and Roll Hall of Fame banquet in New York on March 10, 2008. At the *Espy Awards*, Justin turned on his comedic charm and actually made light of his Super Bowl incident with Janet Jackson. During the performance, he told the audience, "I wanted to be the only guy at a football game to get to second base."[14] During the performance, he also made a jab at David Becham's Tom Ford shoes and acted in a sports-themed opera. Athletes who attended the show were impressed and entertained by Justin's comedic talent. Dallas Cowboys' Terrell Owens said, "He had some funny dialogue; his interaction with the crowd is good. He's an entertainer, and he did a good job."[15] The Espy Awards have been given out since 1993 by the American television station ESPN and actually stand for Excellence in Sports Performance Yearly Awards. Like many other award shows, the host is a contemporary celebrity from pop culture.

He appeared in a commercial for Pepsi during the 2008 Super Bowl. The star could be seen flying over the hood of a car. The ad spot, titled "Magnetic Attraction," was compared to his comedic skits on *SNL*. His *SNL* costar, Andy Samberg, also appeared in the spots with Justin. The ad had Justin doing his own stunts including running into buildings and cars, flying up buildings, taking car doors completely off, and going through the New York Hudson River. His commercial acting includes an ad for Sony where he and Peyton Manning are playing ping-pong. Both he and Manning had to learn some of the words in Chinese for the commercial the two starred in for the Sony Bravia HDTV. One of the commercials also pokes fun at the paparazzi. One of the ads features a cameraman trying to sneak pictures of Justin while hiding in a baby stroller. The commercial is for one of the many Sony cameras. Justin also appears in a marketing campaign for the Audi A1. The commercial only aired in Europe and not in the United States. In November 2009, Justin starred in a perfume commercial for Givenchy's fragrance Play. For the shoot, he traveled to Paris, France, to film the commercial aside the Eiffel Tower. He and an actress are seen trolling the Champ de Mars and then they scale the tower. Paris has been the home of Givenchy since its inception in 1952. Justin was also the spokesperson for Play and Play Intense when the fragrances were released in the United States in September 2009. The first marketing campaign featured newspaper ads and Internet messages. In magazine articles, Justin was asked if he would release a scent of his own as many celebrities have done. In an interview with *Women's Wear Daily* magazine, he said, "I don't know that I would be completely comfortable with a my-name fragrance. It feels like cheating, almost. It doesn't seem like you're creating anything."[16] Justin said there may be a possibility of his William Rast clothing line to put out a scent in the future.

Justin was chosen to announce the 67th annual Golden Globe nominations on December 15, 2009. Together with John Krasinski and Diane Kruger, Justin was pleased to announce the candidates for the 25 categories of the Golden Globes at the Beverly Hilton. Gabourey Sidibe was elated at the sound of her name coming out of Justin's mouth. Sidibe was nominated for Best Actress in a Drama for her work on *Precious*. She had been a fan of 'NSync forever. In an interview with *People* magazine, she said she was ecstatic when the nominees were announced: "Oh my God, Justin Timberlake just said my name. I'm so very excited to come into this because I'm usually on the other side. I'm a fangirl and I watch these things happen, but they don't happen to me!"[17] Emily Blunt, nominated for her role in the film *The Young Victoria*, was not as fortunate with the quip she was given by Justin in her nomination. Blunt was engaged to fellow presenter John Krasinski, so when Blunt's nomination was announced, Justin looked at Krasinski and said, "Somebody's gonna have a good night tonight." The awards are given to those who make great achievements in television and in film. Justin was not nominated for any 2009 Golden Globe Awards.

Not everything Justin has tried has been successful. In trying his hand on Broadway, he auditioned for the part of Roger Davis in *Rent*. He was told that only "Broadway members could convey the true meaning of *Rent*."[18]

Justin has broadened his horizons to include acting to his repertoire. For Justin, it means he has something to do when he needs to take a break from his music career. Although not all his acting endeavors have seen great success, he keeps trying different genres to see where his acting abilities are most profound. Aside from just acting, Justin has also delved into producing and directing. It is this ability to try everything that makes Justin a success in everything he does.

NOTES

1. Hal Marcovitz, *Justin Timberlake: A View from the Paparazzi* (Broomall, PA: Mason Crest Publishers, 2008), p. 50.

2. Clark Collis, "Sexy Beat," *Entertainment Weekly*, February 9, 2007, p. 35.

3. Austin Scaggs, "Justin Timberlake Revs Up His Sex Machine," *Rolling Stone Magazine*, September 21, 2006, p. 54.

4. Jennifer Vineyard, "Why Is Justin Timberlake's *Alpha Dog* Flick So Controversial?" *MTV News*, January 4, 2007, http://www.mtvnews.com.

5. "Timberlake Refused to Take Acting Classes," *World Entertainment News Network*, December 28, 2006, http://wenn.com.

6. Rennie Dyball, "Christina Ricci 'So Impressed' by Justin Timberlake," *People*, March 3, 2007, http://www.people.com.

7. Chris Harris, "Justin Timberlake Will Learn His Lesson in 'Shrek 3,'" *MTV News*, May 2, 2005, http://www.mtvnews.com.

8. "*The Love Guru* Tops Worst Movie of 2008 List," December 3, 2008.

9. "The Elton John Story," *Studio Briefing Film News*, October 13, 2003.

10. Internet Movie Database, http://www.imdb.com.

11. Jocelyn Vena, "Justin Timberlake Wants You to Answer 'The Phone,'" *MTV News*, April 15, 2009, http://www.mtvnews.com.

12. David Sarno, "Timberlake Signs on to Co-Star in Facebook Movie, *The Social Network*," *Los Angeles Times*, September 23, 2009, http://www.latimes.com.

13. "ABC Sports' Singer-Reporter Timberlake May Be 'Sidelined,'" *Studio Briefing Film News*, December 24, 2003.

14. "Timberlake Kicks Off Espy Awards with a Laugh," *World Entertainment New Network*, July 17, 2008, http://wenn.com.

15. Beth Perry, "Justin Timberlake Does 'Great Job' at the ESPYs," *People*, July, 17, 2008, http://www.people.com.

16. Marc Malkin, "Justin Timberlake: Stinkin' Up America, Too!" *E! Online*, July 10, 2009, http://www.eonline.com.

17. Joyce Chen, "Gabourey Sidibe on Globe Nod: Justin Timberlake Said My Name!" *People*, December 15, 2009, http://www.people.com.

18. See http://www.broadwayworld.com.

CHAPTER 6

PERSONALLY SPEAKING

From the time Justin was 11 years old appearing on *Star Search*, his life has been lived in front of cameras, in magazines, and in newspapers. Despite the constant media attention, Justin tries to maintain a private, personal life. "The best thing is that you can reach so many young people with what you do. The worst thing about being famous is probably the invasion of your privacy," Justin said in an interview with *Time for Kids*.[1]

Dating and Justin's relationships have been a hot topic because of his handsome good looks and his celebrity. With only a few long-term relationships during his career, Justin prides himself on being monogamous but also finds himself looking for someone who is like his mom. According to an interview with *Rolling Stone* magazine, he described his relationship with his mother, "She's been my best friend since I figured out who I wanted to be. She's great and such a fun woman. She goes out with me and stays out later than I do. She's always been there beside me, and I think that's part of my problem with girls. You keep searching for someone as good as your mother, and that's a losing battle."[2] Like any other young man, he looks to his mother for the approval of whom he is dating. He believes dating is four to five weeks of people being who they are not just trying to impress the other person. Justin sees himself as a romantic.

Justin's first love interest was Danielle Ditto from his hometown of Millington, Tennessee. Trace Ayala first dated Ditto and introduced Justin and Ditto. The two met at a youth evening at Lucy Church. Ditto also enjoyed singing and sang in talent contests and at the Copper Creek Country Club in Millington. They also shared an importance of church and respectfulness of grandparents. He took Ditto to the Penny Hardaway Classic with his parents. Because Justin was living in Orlando with 'NSync, the long distance became hard. Ditto would sometimes fly in for a weekend or stay weeks at a time. For his 15th birthday, Ditto surprised Justin by hiding in the trunk of his mother's car. Ditto affectionately called Justin a "stud muffin" when at the age of 15 the couple made love. Brian McKnight's "Still in Love" was the couple's song. They were also kicked out of an Orlando recording studio after they were found having sex in the bathroom. The relationship became even more strained when Ditto's grandmother put a stop to the long-distance calls, which were costing up to $600 a month. After Justin's mother, Lynn, walked in on them about to have sex, the pair started to grow apart. Ditto was very well-liked in high school, and although everyone knew she was seeing Justin, she was asked on dates a lot. One particular boy asked her if he could escort her home and she obliged. At the end of the journey, the boy kissed Ditto. After that she could not face Justin, not even talking to him on the phone. The couple grew even more distant. Finally, Ditto mustered up the courage to tell Justin that she had kissed another boy. Infuriated, Justin confronted her at the high school to find out what really happened. Although the two did not break up at that point, their relationship became tense. Ditto finally called him to break it off and have a real life in high school instead of a long-distance relationship. Ditto still has remembrances of Justin, including a treble clef on her ankle and a promise ring she put in her "Justin Memory Box."[3]

Shortly after his breakup with Ditto, Justin began to date Veronica Finn, who was also from Justin's hometown. The two had a lot in common as they both had brothers of a similar age and she grew up close to her grandparents. A singer herself, she was asked to join Lynn's girl band Innosense. Leery at first to join the band because her family wanted her to finish high school, Finn looked to Nikki DeLoach who had already committed to the band. DeLoach also worked with Justin on *The All-New Mickey Mouse Club*. When Finn decided to join the group, she and Justin were already dating. As 'NSync became popular and began to tour constantly, there was less time for a serious relationship commitment. The Innosense group was also on a rigorous schedule to ensure their success. The phone became their only means of communicating as they jetted on tour, beefing up their careers. The Innosense girls were living in the 'NSync house while the band toured in Europe. When they returned the band had to find their own house in Orlando. During the time that both groups were in Orlando, Finn and Justin had a normal dating relationship, going to movies and restaurants. As 'NSync was becoming more and more popular in the United States, the Innosense group was starting their tour in Germany to make a name for themselves. Unfortunately, distance became a large factor and the demise of their courtship. "Doubt became the cancer in their relationship," according to Sean Smith's unauthorized biography.[4]

The next four years of Justin's love life would be consumed by Britney Spears. Lynn has always approved of Spears as she and Justin had known each other since they were 10 years old. The two met on the set of *The All-New Mickey Mouse Club*. Spears and Justin first kissed during their stint with *The All-New Mickey Mouse Club* during a game of truth and dare. In an interview with *Gentleman's Quarterly,* he commented, "I was in love with her from the start. I was infatuated with her from the moment I saw her."[5] In the beginning, the pair denied a relationship to keep their lives private. It was understood that they both had demanding music careers and needed to trust people on their way to stardom. As teenage celebrities too, it could be the demise of their careers and image if it was known that they were involved. In 1999 Justin ranked number one on *People's* list of the "Most Beautiful People of 1999" with Spears listed as number two. For Valentine's Day in 2000, Justin sent her a gift and a note accompanied by a five-piece band playing "The Lady in My Life." For her 17th birthday, Justin had given her a gold ring. Everything that the pair did was scrutinized by the media. The media were constantly speculating about the status of their friendship.

In a May 2000 interview with *Rolling Stone*, Spears broke the silence and said that the couple was dating. After the declaration, Justin's popularity as a musician and a celebrity thrived. The couple was seen all over magazines and newspapers. In the United Kingdom, Justin was affectionately called Mr. Britney. The pair even wore matching outfits to the *American Music Awards* in 2001. Together Spears and Justin soared to the top of the entertainment industry.

In September 2001, burglars broke into the rented home of Spears and Justin. The four burglars stole videos, one of which had personal moments between the couple. The pair had claimed that they were virgins; however, the video allegedly would have made people think differently. They were "concerned that the thieves would sell a copy of the video to the highest bidder, ensuring that the tape would be seen by millions worldwide."[6] Four teenagers were arrested for the break-in, and no form of the video ever surfaced. Eighteen-year-old Matthew Daily, 19-year-olds Salvador Martinez and Marcus Cook, and 20-year-old Richard Olivarez were the offenders who stole videos and also personal items from the home. The items included a cell phone, a hat and scarf, nail polish, and a pair of shoes. The four were sentenced as youthful offenders, so prosecutors asked for 20-month sentences. The sentencing was an agreement reached by both Justin and Spears's lawyers and Circuit Court Judge G. Robert Barron. The judge ordered the perpetrators to sign a confidentiality agreement so the media would not be leaked information as to what was taken from the home. Unfortunately, media outlets obtained the information from the police report.

Justin and Spears waited two years into their relationship to consummate their relationship. Spears revealed their relationship after Justin exposed intimate details of their courtship on television. In a heated interview with *W* magazine, Spears, at the age of 21, said, "I've only slept with one person in my whole life. It was two years into my relationship with Justin and I thought he was the one. But I was wrong. I didn't think he was going to go on Barbara Walters and sell me out."[7]

In March 2002, Spears and Justin split. There were rumors that the tolls on their careers and the fact that they never saw each other caused the breakup. Spears was promoting her new movie *Crossroads* overseas, and Justin was recording and touring with 'NSync. Other reports included infidelity on the part of Spears with choreographer

Wade Robson, who worked with both Justin and Spears. The breakup of this stellar couple was also front-page news. Justin was heartbroken after his relationship with Spears ended. He felt like he was in the middle of a soap opera with all the magazine and tabloids reporting on the story.

Despite Justin's heartache over his split with Spears, the two remain friends. Justin also took a stand when stolen pictures of her newborn son, Sean Preston, were being given to Internet sites and magazines for publication. The whole incident angered Justin to which he stated, "I do think that's crossing the line. That's her baby and those are her baby pictures. It's a little crazy when a person like her, who's obviously a sweet person, and having her first child . . . it's like leave the girl alone, let her have the baby. At some point you're going to get to know about her son and get to see a picture and these magazines work week to week, so I don't understand why people can't wait."[8] Justin has also publicly supported Spears in her drug and alcohol rehabilitation.

Britney Spears, right, star of the film Crossroads, *arrives with her boyfriend Justin Timberlake to the premiere of the film in Los Angeles, February 11, 2002. (AP Photo/Chris Pizzello.)*

He had asked for updates on her condition and progress during her stint at the Promises Rehabilitation Center.

When he was interviewed by Oprah in 2007, aside from talking about his present relationship, Oprah asked about Spears. He didn't comment on Spears's problems but said he hadn't talked to her in years when Oprah pressed him about what he thought was happening in Spears's life. "I think she's a great person, and I don't know her as well as I did. What I do know about her is she has a huge heart, and she is a great person," Justin commented in an interview with Oprah.[9]

Justin was devastated after the breakup with Spears, but as a celebrity heartthrob, there were rumors and speculation that Justin was dating others after the two split. According to United Kingdom magazines, he was in a relationship with singer Kylie Minogue. He was also rumored to be dating Daniele Fisher, Nicole Appleton, and Beyonce Knowles. He met actress Alyssa Milano of *Who's the Boss?* and *Charmed* fame at a Los Angeles bar. The two began dating in September 2002 and split in December. At the 2002 *Grammy Awards*, Justin was spotted with former 'NSync backup dancer Jenna Dewan. For the New Year, he was allegedly seeing Christina Aguilera when they toured together on the *Justified* and *Stripped* tour.

In an interview with *Bop!* magazine, Justin described his ideal girl-friend: "I look for honesty and sensitivity, someone with a sense of humor. And I like independence. It's like she's her own woman, her own person. She's a girl who speaks her mind and takes charge of situations. Oh, and I really dig girls who are into basketball!"[10] He found a fellow Laker fan in April 2003 in Cameron Diaz. He met Diaz at the 2003 Nickelodeon's *Kids' Choice Awards*. Although there was an eight-year difference between the two, they did share a lot in common such as a love for the outdoors. Justin never took his mother's advice of dating around and found a monogamous relationship with Diaz. His decision to keep to himself and not date Diaz in front of the world has made the experience more rewarding. He compares his time with Diaz as being more mature than the time he spent with Spears. In an interview with *People,* he said, "For me, this time around it's been important to stay, at least as much as I can, out of the limelight. And I think that's made it more enriching. I've received so much more from it by keeping it just between the two people it's supposed to be between."[11]

Justin Timberlake performs at the Staples Center in Los Angeles after Christina Aguilera opened their Justified/Stripped *summer concert tour, June 16, 2003. (AP Photo/Kevork Djansezian.)*

During the couple's three-year relationship, there were rumors about the two getting married or splitting up almost constantly. Justin was put on the spot by Ellen DeGeneres when he sang in Central Park for the kickoff of *The Ellen DeGeneres Show*'s fourth season. DeGeneres asked Justin if he was engaged, to which he eventually replied that the pair was not engaged. Justin also replied, "Funny thing, one week we're getting married, one week we've broken up. I can't keep up with it."[12] Justin went on *The Late Show with David Letterman* in 2006 and was asked for the intimate details of his relationship with Diaz. As in many other interviews, Justin refused to give up any information about his personal life. Letterman asked about several things that made Justin uncomfortable including his Super Bowl performance with Janet Jackson and how that really came about, and if Justin did drugs when he was interviewed in Amsterdam by *Rolling Stone*. Being as it was Justin's first time on the show, he was relieved when it was over.

Justin and Diaz vacationed in Hawaii where they laid on the beach and surfed. They were seen golfing, climbing mountains, and attending basketball games together. The relationship ended in December 2006 after three years, and they announced the split on January 11, 2007. To maintain a little bit of privacy in his love life, he asks reporters to submit their questions to his publicist so he can avoid those questions about his love life. Justin is very adamant about his privacy and has publicly admonished the media that try to expose every detail of his personal and professional life. "I despise what they do. They create soap operas out of people's lives. It's a spin game, and I choose not to take part in it," Justin explained in an interview with *Details* magazine.[13]

Despite the on-again, off-again status of Justin's relationships, he is always there for his friends. Even though the pair broke up, Justin attended the funeral of Diaz's father, Emilio Diaz, who died of pneumonia in the spring of 2008.

After his breakup with Diaz, he was speculated to be dating actress and singer Scarlett Johansson. She also appeared in Justin's music video "What Goes Around . . . / . . . Comes Around." Despite reports that Johansson and Justin were linked romantically, Johansson has repeatedly said publicly that the two are just friends. "We have a lot of friends in common, and Justin's a sweetheart, and it's always good to see him but there's a lot of speculation and I try not to read that stuff. I think when two people are single and are seen together, it's immediately like a crazy feeding frenzy," Johansson commented.[14]

In 2007 Justin was linked to actress Jessica Biel. The two were seen at the *Golden Globe Awards* in January. He asked Biel to accompany him on his tour in the United Kingdom. Biel was not only fond of Justin, she was also quite taken with his music. Biel said, "I have to really watch out because I sing Justin's songs at home. When we first started hanging out I had to be really careful because he used to call me and I'd be blasting—and I mean blasting—his music while I was in the pool swimming with my dogs."[15]

Biel also had the opportunity of meeting Justin's mother, Lynn. She found the encounter stressful as is the case with any relationship when someone is meeting the parents for the first time. "It always is a stressful situation. You are always trying—without trying too hard—to be likeable. Y'know mothers and sons and fathers and daughters—those are very protective bonds. So anyone going into that has a tricky situation," Biel said in an interview.[16] Despite trying to be very private about his personal life, in an interview with Oprah in 2007, Justin divulged that he was in fact dating someone. He never mentioned her name on the show but made a reference to his girlfriend smelling lovely. In an appearance on *The Tonight Show with Jay Leno* in 2008, Justin did admit that he was dating Biel. He also told Leno that he was not engaged and was not expecting children as some tabloid magazines reported. Biel never mentioned anything either of the couple's relationship. In an article in *People* magazine, she is quoted as saying, "It's the one part of my life that is my own and not for anyone else."[17]

In early 2009, Justin had bought an apartment in New York. The couple made it known that they were dating to all the fans at the Staples Center for a Lakers game and then explained the incident on *Jimmy Kimmel Live* in 2009. When the Kiss Cam came on and they panned to Dustin Hoffman and his wife, Hoffman gave his wife an opened-mouth kiss. When it was Justin and Biel's turn, the two kissed for a long time. "They cut to Dustin Hoffman and his wife. And he planted an open-mouthed kiss on her that was just kind of award-winning in its own way. And then it cut to us and I was not to be outdone, Okay? So I mounted my girlfriend in front of 18,000 people," he said on the show.[18]

Justin bought an $8.3 million home in Los Angeles in August 2002. He shares the home with his personal assistant and best friend Trace Ayala. Besides a basketball court, the home has video games, pinball machines, and plasma screen TVs. In 2009 he put a putting green in his home so he may practice golf in the comforts of his own home. The cost to convert the room with Astroturf was approximately $800,000.

Justin's appearance has been a constant topic in the media since he started in 'NSync. His hair has been a changing thing starting out as being brown and wiry. He has been seen with his hair in corn rows. Many times he has tried to straighten his hair, but it did not work. When he first cut his curls off, it made newspaper and magazine headlines. During 'NSync, he could be seen wearing T-shirts and baseball caps and then matured into skinny ties and fedora hats. At the age of 19, Justin was considered an American sex symbol. He stayed fit playing basketball; he was charismatic; he had good looks and a winning smile.

A very athletic celebrity, Justin plays basketball and golf in his spare time. Not only does it relax him, it also helps in his charity work. He started golfing when his stepfather, Paul Harless, taught him at the age of 10. He has also been instructed by Tiger Woods' former coach Butch Harmon. Justin tries to play 18 holes twice a week. Justin finds golfing therapeutic and compares it to music, which also has a certain tempo. He has appeared on the cover of *Golf Digest* magazine, a pinnacle of his celebrity career. He was featured with a golf club across his shoulders wearing a fedora and a sweater. The cover was done to coincide with Justin's annual charity events for the Shriners Hospital. After the cover was released, he said, "I'm not going to lie. I mean, I'm done. I don't have to do another magazine cover again."[19] Justin also plays golf with his parents and has admitted that his mother beat him fair and square. In an interview with *People*, Lynn stated, "He took my husband (Paul Harless) and me on a golf trip one time and they were surprised at the end when they added up the scores and I was up on them. I have bragging rights for life."[20] Justin had his first hole in one at a Los Angeles golf course in 2009. It was a par three hole, and he used a Callaway five iron to complete the 185-yard shot. In 2009 he also signed with the company Callaway as a Callaway Golf Staff Professional.

Justin joined the Hollywood basketball team in August 2002. He joined fellow stars Tobey Maguire, Leonardo DiCaprio, and Jaime Foxx. He also enjoys watching the L.A. Lakers and New York Knicks when his schedule allows him to go to the games. Justin also had the tennis courts at his Hollywood Hills home changed into basketball courts. Justin has always been a fan of Michael Jordan and considers him his sports hero. He has one pair of every Air Jordans that were ever made. His favorite color is baby blue because he is a fan of the University of North Carolina Tar Heels.

Justin's singing career received a blow in May 2005 when he needed to have surgery on his throat. After realizing something was wrong with his voice during practices with Snoop Dogg on the song "Signs," he sought medical attention. Doctors diagnosed Justin with nodules, benign growths on his vocal chords, and planned surgery to correct the problem. Many other singers have had the same surgery including Geri Halliwell, Rod Stewart, Julie Andrews, and Joss Stone.

Justin's fame and celebrity has brought him many accolades. In 1999 he made *Teen People* magazine's list of "21 Hottest Stars Under 21." He was voted Most Eligible Bachelor in America in July 2002, and in June 2007 was voted number two in *Elle* magazine's "15 Sexiest Men" poll. In 2002 he was voted one of the Coolest Straight People from *The Advocate*, a gay and lesbian magazine. Justin appeared on the December cover. According to author Sean Smith, "He was accepting his status as a gay icon, as in the music business it is a well-known and accepted premise that a gay fan base is an exceptionally loyal one."[21] *People* magazine voted Justin the trendiest in their 2006 fashion list. The annual compilation lists the best- and worst-dressed celebrities of the year and often equates adjectives to some celebrities. In 2007 Justin was honored with being a Man's Man. In a web site poll by AskMen.com, one million readers participated in the survey. Justin was rated number five behind soccer legend David Beckham, actor Matt Damon, producer Timbaland, and tennis star Roger Federer. The common factor for these celebrity men is the extracurricular activities they take part in. Many of the articles pertaining to the celebrities report more than just their career accomplishments but also foundations, charities, and companies that they help out in their free time.

In December 2007, he made Barbara Walters' list of "The 10 Most Fascinating People of the Year." He shared the honor with J. K. Rowling, former president Bill Clinton, Hugo Chavez, Venezuelan president, Victoria and David Beckham, actresses Katherine Heigl and Jennifer Hudson, Don Imus, and MySpace founders Tom Anderson and Chris DeWolfe. By both *People* and *Cosmopolitan* magazines, Justin had made the list of one of the sexiest men, losing to Matt Damon in the *People* poll. In 2008 he was named number two on the "Richest Stars Under 30" by *Forbes* magazine, second only to singer Beyonce Knowles. His estimated worth is $43 million. He was also ranked 28th in 2008 in *Entertainment Weekly's* "30 Under 30" list. At the *People's Choice Awards* on January 8, 2008, Justin was honored with being one of the nominees for the Favorite Star Under 35 award, a new category to celebrate the 35th anniversary of *People* magazine. Other musicians also nominated were Rihanna, Beyonce Knowles, Taylor Swift, and Carrie Underwood. Underwood was the winner of the first time award. Aside from being a good singer and celebrity, Justin is also recognized for his wardrobe.

In 2009 he was named on GQ's "10 Most Stylish Men in America." Justin attributes his dapper dress to his stepfather, Paul Harless, who almost always wears dress shirts and ties. His hats and skinny ties have also been compared to the style of Michael Jackson. Justin shared the accolade with singers Mark Ronson, T. I., and Kanye West. In a poll put together by PopEater, Justin was named one of the biggest stars of the decade of 2000s. Spears, Justin's former girlfriend, was named the biggest celebrity of the decade, followed by Jolie, Beyonce, and then Justin. Paris Hilton and Tom Cruise followed Justin in the poll. The voting was done online by fans of PopEater. Not only does he inspire other musicians and celebrities, Justin was the inspiration behind an art gallery showing by artist Nicholas Weist in 2008. The exhibit was titled "If I Told You You Were Beautiful Would You Date Me on the Regular?" and was shown at the Oliver Kamm 5BE Gallery in New York. The presentations were made of photography, sculptures, and installations.

Although Justin admits that he is shy and doesn't like talking to people he doesn't know, he has made a great impact on the celebrity world.

NOTES

1. Jillian Klueber, "Justin's Solo Act," *Time for Kids*, November 11, 2002, http://www.timeforkids.com.

2. Eric Hedegaard, "The Bachelor," *Rolling Stone Magazine*, January 23, 2003, p. 34.

3. Sean Smith, *Justin: The Unauthorized Biography* (New York: Pocket Books, 2004), pp. 74–76.

4. Smith, *Justin*, p. 110.

5. Lisa DePaulo, "Locked and Loaded," *Gentlemen's Quarterly*, August 2006, p. 116.

6. "Britney's Pure Reputation May Be Soiled," *World Entertainment News Network*, September 27, 2001.

7. "Britney Spears: 'I've Only Slept with Justin,'" *World Entertainment News Network*, July 9, 2003.

8. "Timberlake: 'Let's Wait for Britney's Baby Pictures,'" *San Francisco Chronicle*, October 25, 2005.

9. Stephen M. Silverman, "Justin Timberlake Opens Up about His Love Life," *People*, September 19, 2007.

10. Martin Roach, *Justin Timberlake: The Unofficial Book* (London: Virgin Books, 2003), p. 30.

11. Marla Lehner, "Justin Says He Was 'Infatuated' with Britney," *People*, July 19, 2006.

12. Stephen M. Silverman, "Justin on Cameron: 'We're Not Engaged,'" *People*, September 4, 2006.

13. "Timberlake Hits Out at Celebrity Culture," *San Francisco Chronicle*, April 4, 2007.

14. "Johansson: 'I'm Not Dating Timberlake,'" *World Entertainment News Network*, February 13, 2007.

15. Laura Martin, "Biel: 'I Listen to Justin's Music,'" *Digital Spy*, December 30, 2008.

16. "Biel Was 'Stressed' Meeting Timberlake's Mother," *World Entertainment News Network*, November 5, 2008.

17. Kate Stroup, "Jessica Biel Considers Justin Her Private Present," *People*, December 9, 2008.

18. Brian Orloff, "Justin Timberlake Explains Courtside PDA with Jessica Biel," *People*, April 23, 2009.

19. Simon Reynolds, "Biel 'Takes Up Golf for Timberlake,'" *Digital Spy*, December 29, 2008.

20. Mark Gray, "Justin Timberlake's Mom Beats Him at Golf," *People*, October 16, 2009.

21. Smith, *Justin*, p. 204.

CHAPTER 7

"FOLLOW MY LEAD"

Because of his success, Justin realizes as a celebrity he has the means
to give back to communities both monetarily and through his talents.
He also realizes his ventures do not have to be limited to music and
acting.

During his years with 'NSync, Justin participated in JC Chasez's
foundation Challenge for the Children. Every year there was a basketball game held to raise money for various charities. In 1999, more than
$50,000 was raised. In 2000 the event was held at St. John's University
in New York. More than $100,000 was donated to the Arnold Palmer
Hospital. His basketball career also includes playing with children at
the Ronald McDonald House.

In 2001 the Justin Timberlake Foundation was established through
the Giving Back Fund. The Giving Back Fund was created in 1997 to
promote celebrities giving back to charities, matches celebrities up with
charities, and establishes celebrity charities and foundations. Justin's
foundation concentrates on bringing music into schools. The foundation began shortly after the 1999 Columbine High School shootings.
Justin believes that hostilities can be released through music. Learning
music also helps children achieve their full potential. The first grant

was given to Justin's hometown school, E. E. Jeter Elementary School. The school received a donation of $50,000 for their "Music in Education" program. The grant helped fund 16 keyboards, percussion instruments, winds, and a building to house everything in. Free piano lessons were also provided to the community. In 2002 the foundation partnered with the American Music Conference. The pair promoted music education in secondary schools. Justin also used MTV's *Total Request Live* television show to urge viewers to get involved in music education. He believes that no matter what a student decides for a career, they should be able to enjoy music in schools. Justin also prompted students 13 and older to write their Congressional representatives about saving school music programs. They also lobbied the U.S. Congress to fund music programs in schools. For his continuing support to give back to where he came from and for promoting music education in schools, Justin was honored by the White House.

Golf has also become a personal and professional outlet for Justin as he uses charity golf events to raise money and takes time out of his schedule for a leisurely game now and then. "I love golf because of my situation with work, all over the place, all of the time. Playing golf, you're in one place for four and a half or five hours. I can be myself," Justin commented.[1]

In January 2002, he played the Bob Hope Classic in Palm Springs. He hosted the Professional Golf Association's charity open for the Shriners Hospital. According to the organization's web site, "Shriners Hospital for Children is an international health care system of 22 hospitals dedicated to improving the lives of children by providing pediatric specialty care, innovative medical research and teaching programs. Children up to the age of 18 with orthopedic conditions, burns, spinal cord injuries, and cleft lip and palate conditions are eligible for care and receive all services at no charge—regardless of financial need."[2]

Justin signed a five-year contract with the Shriners Hospital to host the event. The event is now called the Justin Timberlake Shriners Hospital for Children Open. Forty professional golfers and 13 celebrities participated in the tournament. Professional golfers for the 2008 tournament included John Daly, Bob Estes, and Mark Hensby. Former 'NSync member Chris Kirkpatrick, comedian George Lopez, and swimmer Amanda Beard were among the celebrities that turned out. Justin asked

'NSync singer Justin Timberlake blasts out of a trap on the 17th hole at the Bob Hope Chrysler Classic, January 15, 2002, at Indian Wells Country Club in Indian Wells, California. (AP Photo/Mark J. Terrill.)

for help from celebrities by just plain asking them without the usual fanfare associated with celebrities. In an interview with *People* magazine he commented that he asked his friends the "old-fashioned" way. "I actually wrote letters. I was old fashioned. I didn't have to stalk anyone."[3] In November 2008, Justin released the single, "Follow My Lead." The song was released on Justin's MySpace page with all download fees benefiting the Shriners Children's Hospital. The single was recorded live at the Justin Timberlake & Friends Concert in October 2008.

At "Justin Timberlake and Friends: A Special Evening Benefiting the Shriners Hospital for Children," Justin brought together several musical acts, including 50 Cent, the Jonas Brothers, Lionel Ritchie, Adam Levine, Rihanna, Boys II Men, Leona Lewis, and will.i.am. Together with Ritchie and will.i.am, Justin sang the Commodores' song "Easy" as well as a duet with Levine. Justin retired his 2006 hit "SexyBack" at the concert. He also proclaimed that he was working on his collaborations with other artists rather than his solo career.

In October 2009, Justin put together his second annual charity concert to coincide with the golf tournament, called the Justin Timberlake & Friends Concert. It took place at Mandalay Bay Hotel & Casino in Las Vegas, Nevada, to benefit the Shriners Hospital for Children. Among the musicians taking part included TLC, Snoop Dogg, Timbaland, Jay Sean, and Taylor Swift. The last two remaining members of the group TLC, Tione (T-Bone) Watkins and Rozonda (Chilli) Thomas, also played at the concert. It was the first time in seven years that the group played in the United States. Lisa "Left Eye" Lopes, the third member of the band, was killed in a car accident in 2002. Justin played emcee, singer, and maestro for the night including giving the audience the Yankees/Angels baseball score during musical acts. After three hours, the night ended successfully. Justin's band members had been on stage for the whole night. The concert is preceded by golfing, a golf clinic for children, a celebrity golf tournament, and then the concert at Mandalay Bay. One of the biggest parts of the tournament is the Wives Luncheon, which Justin's mother, Lynn, put together. The lunch is to bring together those whose spouses are playing in the celebrity tournament. Both Justin and Lynn found that none of the other tournaments do anything for the wives and realized what a supportive group of people they are.

At the end of 2009, Justin was named Top Philanthropist of the Year for his work with the Shriners Hospital. In 2009 he raised $9.3 million for the organization. Out of 50 celebrities listed on *The Daily Beast* web site, Justin was ranked number one. He was followed by Madonna who raised $5.5 million for the foundation Raising Malawi. Other musicians on the list included Rihanna, Shakira, and Bono.

Justin also donates his musical talents as well to help those in need. On July 30, 2003, he participated in the Toronto Rocks SARS event, at Toronto's Downsview Park, with The Rolling Stones. "Estimated to have between 450,000 and 500,000 people attending the concert, it is the largest outdoor ticketed event in Canadian history, and one of the largest in North American history."[4] Unfortunately for Justin the audience did not take kindly to him on the stage when he sang "Cry Me a River," "Señorita," and "Rock Your Body." The crowd threw empty water bottles at him while he was on stage. Before leaving the stage, Justin politely thanked the city of Toronto and did come back to sing with Mick Jagger on the song "Miss You." Rolling Stones guitarist Keith Richards reprimanded the audience when they began again throwing water bottles at Justin.

He sang with James Brown in 2005 to raise money for those affected by the Asian tsunami. At the Grammy Awards on February 13, 2005, Justin was given an award for his philanthropy in Tennessee. Memphis native and director Craig Brewer also received the award during the Grammys. To help victims of Hurricane Katrina in 2006, Justin donated money to the cause from sales of his songs on iTunes. To give back to where he came from, Justin donated $200,000 to Memphis in 2008. One half of the money went to the Rock 'n' Soul Museum in Memphis and the other half went to the Memphis Music Foundation. Justin gives back to his hometown because Memphis music has been an important influence in his life and in his career. John Doyle, the executive director of the Memphis Rock 'n' Soul Museum stated, "Justin Timberlake has never deserted Memphis, Tennessee. He has never stopped giving back to the community, to the local music industry, and to young people."[5]

Justin has participated in the "MTV Staying Alive," which began in 1998. The initiative is an international campaign that encourages youth to speak about the illness and to educate young people of the risks of HIV and AIDS. It is also used to fight off the stigma and discrimination of HIV and AIDS. The annual show began as a documentary with six youth talking about their affliction, with George Michael hosting the program. In 2002 the campaign went global, and in 2005 a foundation was set up for those afflicted by HIV and AIDS. Several other musicians have helped in the efforts including Beyonce Knowles, Kanye West, Mary J. Blige, and P. Diddy.

In December 2000, Justin joined other celebrities to protest the current gun laws in America. Together with Uma Thurman, Melanie Griffith, Michael Douglas, and others, he posed for a photo for Marie Claire's End Gun Violence Now. The celebrities donned "campaign T-shirts and joined hands to demonstrate their united front against arms."[6]

Michael Jackson had commissioned Justin to sing on the charity track "What More Can I Give." The recording was to raise money for families affected by the September 11 tragedy. He was to perform with singers Mariah Carey, Ricky Martin, Celine Dion, and Beyonce Knowles.

There are many charities that Justin donates to as well including Childwatch, a group that prevents childhood abductions, and Wildlife Warriors Worldwide, an organization founded by the late Crocodile Hunter, Steve Irwin. In late 2007, Justin donated $100,000 to the Wildlife Foundation. While on his *FutureSex/LoveShow* Tour in Australia, he told his audience that he would donate the money at a concert in Brisbane. Irwin gave Justin a personal tour of the foundation, which moved Justin to make the donation. The charity was created to protect and conserve wildlife and the environment. Other charities Justin supports include Mercy Corps Mission Australia, MusiCares, and OxFam. To raise funds for music education programs he also became the spokesman for MathNMusic Club for Youth, an online educational music campaign.

At the Keep A Child Alive Black Ball in November 2008, Justin shared the stage with fellow singer Alicia Keys. The couple sang "Another Day in Paradise," while Justin sang "Love Stoned/I Think She Knows" and "Until the End of Time." Both Keys and Justin share a common goal of helping the children of Africa. The Keep Children Alive foundation improves access to therapy and money provides nutritional services, diagnostic testing, and provides sites where children of AIDS can be cared for in Africa, and was founded by singer Alicia Keys.

After a fan was killed outside of a radio station by a drunken driver, Justin became the spokesman for an anti-drunk-driving campaign. Cameron Duty, 23 years old, supposedly got into an altercation with a person in the crowd on September 9, 2002. He got into his vehicle and backed his truck into a group of Justin's fans. One 21-year-old fan, Anna White from Bellevue, Washington, was killed. She was standing outside on a sidewalk in front of the Burbank, California, radio station, KIIS-FM. A crowd of fans were waiting to catch a glimpse of Justin after his interview. After Duty's truck hit White, she became pinned underneath the truck and was dragged for a block. Duty was arrested on charges of drunken driving, murder, and hit-and-run. Duty pled not guilty to the charge of murder in 2002. He was placed under arrest on $1 million bail. On October 29, 2002, he had a preliminary hearing in Pasadena Superior Court. According to documents and news reports, officers stated that Duty did not previously know White before the in-cident.[7] To alert young people to the dangers of drinking and driving, Justin joined the group RADD, Recording Artists, Actors and Ath-letes Against Drunk Driving. He wrote and produced television ads for an anti-drunk-driving campaign. Justin explained his involvement in RADD, stating, "The senseless death of Anna White yet again dem-onstrates the horrors of drunk driving. I can only hope that partnering with RADD will raise awareness and convince others never to drive after they've had even a few drinks."[8]

On September 5, 2008, Justin was part of the *Fashion Rocks* concert at Radio City Music Hall in New York City. Together with singers Be-yonce, Keith Urban, Mariah Carey, and Kid Rock, Justin performed with the proceeds benefiting Stand Up for Cancer. The concert com-bines music and the fashions of the time. The fifth annual event was a two-hour special that aired on CBS.

Justin Timberlake performs onstage during Condé Nast's Fashion Rocks *show, September 5, 2008, in New York.* (*AP Photo/Jeff Christensen.*)

In the spring of 2009, Justin climbed Mount Kilimanjaro for a charity event called "Summit on the Summit." The goal was to raise funds to raise awareness of the water shortage in developing countries in what is called the Children's Safe Drinking program. Both he and actress Jessica Biel participated in the event in 2010. By 2009 more than 1.8 billion liters of clean water had been distributed worldwide.

Ten O'Clock Classics, a nonprofit organization that provides children with music lessons and instruments, was a recipient of Justin's generosity in September 2009. Jon Biel, the father of actress Jessica Biel, showed Justin a newspaper article about the group and knew that music in schools was a cause that Justin was very fond of. Justin signed a baby grand piano to be auctioned off with the proceeds going to Ten O'Clock Classics. Singer and songwriter Billy Joel also signed a piano for the organization. The organization has a similar mission to the Justin Timberlake Foundation that fund-raises to keep music programs in schools. Ronen Segev, the founder of Ten O'Clock Classics, said, "He cares about music education and wants to make sure these kids can continue to have music lessons."[9] In 2009 Comcast and the Stand Up to Cancer organization joined forces to release Stand Up 2 Cancer on Demand. The special is designed to raise funds for cancer awareness and cancer research. Justin was one of the entertainers featured on the special, which included hundreds of music videos from various musicians. Other performers included Alicia Keys, Lady Gaga, Sting, Bon Jovi, and Mariah Carey. Justin also appeared in a commercial campaign in which celebrities write slogans on a large white wall to raise awareness of the disease. Actress Renee Zellweger led the campaign with Rob Lowe and Kristin Chenoweth.

Leonardo DiCaprio recruited Justin for a public service ad in October 2008. The promotional ad was made to encourage people to go to the polls and vote. It encouraged the public to find "Five More Friends" and go vote. Among the celebrities who also participated in the campaign were Tom Cruise, Snoop Dogg, Steven Speilberg, Julia Roberts, and Harrison Ford. Internet sites MySpace and Google also urged young people to make a difference and vote.

Biel and Justin also supported the Obama presidential campaign in 2008. During a rally at the Clark County Government Center amphitheater in Las Vegas, Justin urged voters to get out and cast their ballots for the Democratic nominee. Justin had never publicly endorsed a candidate before. At the Last Chance for Change rally, the pair claimed they were not present as celebrities but as Americans. Justin told the crowd on October 11, 2008, "This is not my usual stage . . . and I'm a little nervous. This is the first time in my life that I am endorsing a political candidate. I'm not here as a musician or an actor or that guy that writes songs. I'm not here as a Democrat or a Republican, I'm here as an America."[10]

Justin played presenter for the first *TeenNick HALO Awards* on December 11, 2009. Nick Cannon founded the award show. He presented awards with Alicia Keys, Hayden Panettiere, and LeBron James. The awards were given to four teenagers who give back to their communities in a positive way. The teenagers were involved in an AIDS education organization, a group for ocean research, a drug and gang awareness program, and a girls group for those who suffer from scoliosis. The winners get to help their celebrity with their own fund-raiser. Leah Stoltz, who won for forming a scoliosis support group, was teamed up with Justin.

Justin was invited to sing at the first annual Show of Peace Concert in Beijing at the Bird's Nest Stadium. Rick Garson, the producer of the show, is a television and music producer from the company ZZYX Entertainment. The concert was a tribute to the cultural exchange agreement between the United States and China; 2010 marks the 30th anniversary of the pact. Other organizations that helped put the project together were Chinese People's Association for Friendship with Foreign Countries, the Joint U.S.-China Collaboration on Clean Energy, the United Nations' Pathways of Peace and the Captain Planet Foundation. Many other artists were invited to perform including Beyonce, Coldplay, and the Black Eyed Peas.

In order to raise money and become a celebrity influence, Justin has to prove his success. He has done this through not only his musical and acting talents but also his business savvy. His first business venture was a club in California in 2003 called the Chi Club, located in the Hyatt Hotel on Sunset Boulevard. He partnered with Art and Allan Davis. This venture into the food service world expanded in February 2006 when he helped Eytan Sugarman open Destino in New York. It is known as "one of the premiere Southern Italian restaurants in Manhattan."[11] Chef Mario Curko, a Croatian immigrant, prides himself on knowing what goes best in Italian cuisine. As the executive chef Destino's, Curko has also worked at several other popular New York restaurants including Pietro's, Christ Cella, Tre Scalini, and Scarlatti. Another restaurant, Southern Hospitality, opened in March 2007. Trace Ayala and Eytan Sugarman are partners in the restaurant. The décor is meant to depict distinct places in Tennessee. Memorabilia on the wall are from well-known Southern musicians including Johnny Cash, Hank Williams, Jerry Lee Lewis, and Elvis Presley. The cuisine is pulled pork sandwiches, ribs, chicken, catfish, and other Southern dishes. With flat screen televisions and a beer-pong table, Southern Hospitality is a popular spot for celebrities and local New Yorkers.

Justin's own tequila brand is 901, the name chosen because it is the area code of his hometown in Memphis. While at the club Lavo in Las Vegas, Justin bought everyone in the club a shot of his new liquor. The alcohol is homegrown in Mexico. In an effort to involve the public in the marketing of the liquor, on the 901 web site, there was a contest for the best marketing idea. The winner received a $25,000 signing bonus, a trip to Las Vegas for the annual Justin and Friends Concert for the Shriners Hospital, and was named Executive Vice President of Big Ideas for 901. Malachi Rempen, a filmmaker from Albuquerque, New Mexico, won the 901 tequila contest. His campaign, with the catch phrase, "Only one way your night shall begin," won among all the entries. When the tequila originally came out it was only available in New York, Los Angeles, Las Vegas, and St. Louis.

Jay Tee Records was formed in 2005. However, in 2007 he started another record label with Interscope Records called Tennman Records. The Jay Tee Record label is an exclusive part of Tennman Records and no artists have been signed to that label. Justin is the Chief Executive Officer and Chairman of the company. The company's president is Ken Komisar; Chief Operating Officer is Rey Flemings; and Navin Watumull is the company's A&R manager. Another new artist signed to the label was Matt Morris, a musician who had written songs for Justin's second solo album. "The company's goal is to bring new talent to the public," according to author Tony Napoli.[12]

The first singer that the label looked at was Dutch Esmee Denters, who was gaining popularity through YouTube videos. Denters was born September 28, 1988, in Westervoort, the Netherlands. Her father was a lawyer and her mother was a secretary. She was attending the HAN University of Applied Sciences where she was studying to become a social worker until she quit in February 2007. Denters shot her own video with her Webcam and had put it on YouTube in August 2006. She sang songs from Beyonce, Alicia Keys, and Alanis Morrisette. Her video received more than 21 million hits. She is also credited as being the "first unsigned singer in history to go directly from personal YouTube postings to commercially performing on a major stage."[13] Dutch artist Jonathan Berhane saw the video on YouTube and contacted the singer. Berhane in turn led her to Billy Mann, a songwriter and manager who has worked with such artists as Pink, Ricky Martin, Backstreet Boys, and Celine Dion. Mann introduced her to Justin at one of his concerts. She attributes Justin for helping to make her dreams come true and realizing her potential.[14] During the summer of 2007, Denters received the privilege of performing with Justin in his summer concert series and played 10 venues in Europe. In 2008, Denters and Justin recorded "Follow My Lead." The song was only available through download on MySpace. All monies from the project were donated to the Shriners Hospitals for Children.

Denters's first album, *Outta Here*, was released January 11, 2010. The album is heavily influenced by Justin who helped Denters rework some of the lyrics and harmonies. Justin gave her advice through the process on how to put herself into the music. Denters's foray into the music world was singing other people's songs on YouTube. Her first album was designed to be her mark on the music business. "We sat down and he went through all the songs I'd written and changed some of the production and lyrics. Later on I actually started writing with him, which was amazing because it was so one-on-one and we got along really well. He was very open to what I wanted, because at the end of the day it's my record," according to Denters's web site.[15]

In September 2009, Justin was looking to sign another young talent named Justin Bieber. Bieber, like Denters, posted his videos on YouTube for the world to see and also had a collection of fans on Twitter.

Unfortunately for Tennman Records Usher also looked to sign the young pop music star. In the end, Bieber signed with Usher's label. Other artists recording under the Tennman Record label include Free Sol and Brenda Radney.

Justin and Trace Ayala also brought to the public a new line of hip clothes, called William Rast, in October 2006. The name came from both Justin and Ayala's grandfathers names. The clothes range from men and women's items and can be bought in high-end stores such as Nordstrom and Bloomingdales. The pair hired Johan and Marcella Lindeberg to manage their clothing line. The two launched a golf label called J. Lindeberg. During New York's Fashion Week in February 2009, Justin, along with the Lindebergs, showcased the new line of William Rast clothing. Justin is the idea man, bringing together different types of cultures, eras, and styles in his clothing line. In an interview with MTV News, Justin explained his role at the company, "The way I work with them is give them ideas on lifestyle. Not so much specific clothing cause that's what they're so good at—taking a general idea and throwing it into specifics and making it a part of the clothing; that is that lifestyle."[16] Justin also participated in Fashion's Night Out during Fashion Week in 2009. The event, which featured Justin and other celebrities, was designed to get people shopping in the stores amid a weak economy. Retail stores were the hardest hit during the recession in 2009 and retail sales declined every month during the year. William Rast added two new retail stores and an outlet store to expand their business in 2009. Stores opened in Westfield Century City Shopping Mall in Los Angeles, California, and at the Valley Fair Shopping Mall in San Jose, California. The outlet store opened at the Desert Hills Premium Outlets in Cabazon, California. The goal for the company is to open at least 40 to 50 retail stores in the next few years.

To promote the Willam Rast line of denim wear, Justin himself made several commercials as the fictional character William Rast. In the ad, he claims he is a hero, saying, "My name is William Rast, a complex modern day hero, who rebels against the conformity of everyday life." Model Erin Wasson plays Birdie, Rast's girlfriend. The two are donning Rast clothes as they adventure around Tennessee. The ads were featured in print, on billboards, and in film. Aside from starring in the ads, Justin wrote the ads and provided the music and lyrics.

In 2009 he was honored with being on the *Gentleman's Quarterly* list of most stylish men. Again it wasn't because he was a trendsetter but because he wears the style well. "Timberlake has a knack for targeting trends just before they crest. He might not spark them, but he's the guy who broadcasts them—whom we point to for making, say, hats popular again, or for making suits look like they were *meant* to be worn with sneakers, or for wearing a beard that's not quite a beard per se but is pretty much what every guy at the club wears these days," according to an article in *Gentleman's Quarterly* magazine.[17]

Justin's love for basketball has furthered his ventures into writing and playing on a team. He is a member of the NBA Entertainment League. This is made up of about 130 celebrities with 12 different teams. Some of the players include Tobey Maguire, Leonardo DiCaprio, Woody Harrelson, and David Arquette. In 1999 fellow musician Brian McKnight was named as 1999 MVP for the league.

Inside Drive: A Novel of Basketball, Life and Love was written by Justin and published in the United Kingdom in March 2003. It was about Justin Taylor who played for the Tampa Stingrays and a girl who played point guard on the team. The book deal was scrapped by publisher Ballantine Books in 2001 because Justin did not have time to go on book and promotional tours. In an interview with the Associated Press, a representative from Ballantine Books said, "We felt very strongly that we needed him to be able to go out on the road and do national media appearances and bookstore events."[18] Justin's publicist cited the reason he was not available at that time was because he had too many other projects going on. ABC Sports made Justin a special correspondent, but he found that his commentary was more fan based than analysis based. The NBA also used his musical talents in their ad campaign "Can't Get Enough."

Justin combined his love for golf with his love for the environment. He bought the Mirimichi Golf Course in Tennessee and renovated the course to make it eco-friendly. The term *Mirimichi* means "place of happy retreat" in the Native American language. The total renovation cost $16 million. He was the first to play 18 holes on the course. He started at 7:30 A.M. and played a foursome with his mother, stepfather, and a family friend. In an interview with the Tennessee newspaper, *The Commercial Appeal*, Justin describes the endeavor as "probably the coolest thing I've ever been a part of in my life."[19] Of the 200 acres of the golf course, only 85 of them are used for the golf course. It was named a "classic sanctuary" by Audubon International. Justin's dad encouraged him to buy the Memphis, Tennessee golf course in 2007, making Lynn and Paul Harless and Justin partners in the project.

The golf course was closed January 15 to July 17, 2010, to make improvements. The greens, bunkers, and drainage ditches were improved. The floral and fauna of the course was also expanded. Although Justin did not want to close the course, he thought it would be better than making gradual improvements over the next three years.[20]

With all the personal projects that Justin has on his plate, he still makes time for his music career. He has touched the lives of many people with all his fundraising efforts and entrepreneurial ventures. The personal projects and giving back positively to the community is a large part of what Justin has grown his celebrity to be.

NOTES

1. Sean Smith, *Justin: The Unauthorized Biography* (New York: Pocket Books, 2004), p. 168.

2. Shriners Hospital for Children, http://www.shrinershq.com.

3. Mark Gray, "Inside Justin Timberlake & Pals $1M Fundraiser," *People*, October 22, 2008, http://www.people.com.

4. "Molson Canadian Rocks for Toronto," Fact-Archive.com, http://www.cbc.ca/news/background/sarsbenefit/.

5. Janet Mock, "Justin Timberlake Donates $200,000 to His Hometown," *People*, March 24, 2008.

6. "Stars Join Forces to Ban Guns," *World Entertainment News Network*, December 4, 2000.

7. Stephen M. Silverman, "Timberlake Fan's Death: Murder Charge," *People*, September 12, 2002.

8. Stephen M. Silverman, "Not Guilty Plea in 'NSync Fan Death," *People*, September 27, 2002.

9. "Justin Timberlake in Sync with Kid's Charity," *People*, September 28, 2009.

10. Robin Leach, "Justin Timberlake Hosts 'Last Chance for Change' Rally," *Las Vegas Sun*, October 11, 2008.

11. http://www.destinony.com.

12. Tony Napoli, *Justin Timberlake: Breakout Music Superstar*. Hot Celebrity Biographies. (Berkley Heights, NJ: Enslow Publishers, 2010), p. 39.

13. See http://www.esmeeworld.com.

14. Stephen M. Silverman, "Justin Timberlake Signs YouTube Singer to His Label," *People*, June 5, 2007.

15. David Balls, "Denters Album 'Has Timberlake Imprint,'" *Digital Spy News*, December 15, 2009.

16. Jocelyn Vena, "Justin Timberlake's William Rast Makes Fashion Week Debut," *MTV News*, February 18, 2009.

17. Adam Rappaport, "Justin Timberlake," *Gentlemen's Quarterly*, March 2009.

18. Gary Susman, "'Inside' Out," *E! Online*, October 30, 2001.

19. John Belfuss, "Mirimichi Golf Course Is 'the Coolest Thing' Timberlake Has Ever Done," *The Commercial Appeal*, July 24, 2009.

20. "Singer Justin Timberlake Closing New Memphis Golf Course for 6 Months for Renovation," Associated Press, December 16, 2009.

CHAPTER 8

CONTROVERSY

As hard as celebrities try to give back to their communities and try to maintain a "normal" life, because of constant media attention and scrutiny, it can be hard not to be seen negatively. Justin also has had his negative spotlight moments during his career with 'NSync, such as his many relationships that have been strewn in the newspapers and magazines, his historic wardrobe malfunction at the 2004 Super Bowl, various lawsuits throughout the years, and several altercations with the media in regard to his private life. Although Justin tries to avoid the tabloids, he knows that with promoting himself comes scrutiny: "You sort of know it exists because, the more promotion you do, the more you hear about it. But if I wasn't doing all this promotion, I wouldn't even know about it. I'd be surfing or snowboarding or playing golf. That's how I keep my sanity. You cannot do this without a sense of humor. Otherwise you get caught pleasuring yourself in a bathroom stall."[1]

Justin's first negative incident came on November 19, 2000, when 'NSync was performing a concert in St. Louis, Missouri. Among the fans trying to get a look at the band after the show was 15-year-old Danielle McGuire. As the band tried to push through the mobbing crowd, it was believed that Justin was snubbing fans after the concert.

McGuire did not like the attitude that Justin had at the time, so she allegedly retorted that she liked JC better.

Bodyguards of Justin brought the 15-year-old girl to Justin's hotel room where he allegedly berated and intimidated her. According to the lawsuit, McGuire suffered from "fright, shock, intimidation, severe emotional distress, bodily harm, embarrassment, humiliation and distress."[2] The McGuires were seeking damages of more than $25,000. In light of the lawsuit, both 'NSync and Justin's reputation were tarnished. Reports were referring to Justin as an egotistical superstar who was rude to fans and ignored autograph requests. Eventually, the charges were dropped against Justin, and the lawsuit never went to court. John S. Wallach, McGuire's attorney, revealed that 'NSync fans were giving McGuire a hard time at school and one girl was supposedly suspended for making threats, stated Sean Smith in his biography.[3]

Justin was sued by his former tour manager, Ibrahim Duarte, for $9.6 million. Duarte filed a claim in New York Supreme Court in November 2003. He claimed that Justin and members of 'NSync were allegedly constantly making racial slurs against him; Darrin Henson, their choreographer; and Dale Ramsey, a sound engineer. He was the band's tour manager for their *No Strings Attached* Tour from January 1999 to December 2000. Duarte also alleges that he was fired as the tour manager for racial reasons and replaced by a white manager who did not have the experience that he had. Ironically, 'NSync, at the time, was managed by Wright Entertainment Group, head by Johnny Wright, an African American. According to an article from MTV *News*, the lawsuit named members of 'NSync, Zeeks Inc., Skeez LLC and 'NSYNC Inc., the band's holding companies.[4] Supposedly, Bass also made Duarte ride in a separate tour bus because he was ashamed of having a black manager. Duarte claimed, "After four years of building them into one of the hottest bands in the world, they treated me less than human. The popularity and money went to their heads and their true feelings about having a black front man became apparent. I endured their constant racial slurs, jokes, and belittling comments to make it work. But they just threw me to the curb like yesterday's trash."[5] Duarte had been in the music business for 25 years and claims he had never been treated as badly as he was with the band 'NSync. In June 2002, he had filed a suit against the band for back pay that he never received.

Justin's relationship with Britney Spears was also not safe from the tabloids. Between the pair saying they were just friends to admitting that they were in a relationship, the couple was seen as a great celebrity entity called "Timberspears." The tabloids got it wrong and the world was shocked when it was reported that the two had gotten into a car accident. Supposedly, Spears was killed and Justin was in a coma after the accident. In reality the two were on two different coasts with Spears in Los Angeles and Justin in Philadelphia. Justin first called Spears to make sure she was okay. Justin was outraged that someone would put his family through a falsehood like claiming he was dead. Immediately after the story broke, Justin received a barrage of phone calls from his family and friends. Justin said, "Since the beginning, (of) our relationship, there's always been things that have been said that were totally not true. But this just, like, took it to a whole 'nother planet."[6] After statements from their publicists that the musicians were fine, it was found that the story was a hoax. The story was reported by Dallas radio station KEGL-FM. The radio personalities, Kramer and Twitch, found the report on a Los Angeles news source and allegedly Cedars Sinai Medical Center confirmed the report. No formal complaints were made against the radio station to the FCC. The two disc jockeys were fired from the station, according to *Billboard* magazine.[7]

Justin's biggest controversy of his career was his half-time performance at Super Bowl XXXVIII on February 1, 2004, with fellow musician Janet Jackson. The game was between the New England Patriots and the Carolina Panthers in Houston, Texas. Originally Justin turned down the opportunity to perform until Janet Jackson personally asked Justin to do the half-time show with her. He flew in from Spain where he was performing on tour. "I've been on tour for the past three months and I got a call from my manager to do the Super Bowl. I initially turned it down. Then I got a call from Janet and decided to do it. We found a way to work the performance into one musically, her song going into mine," Justin commented after the incident.[8] Other artists that performed at the Super Bowl were Kid Rock, Sean "P. Diddy" Combs, and Nelly Furtado.

MTV promised the more than 140 television viewers, both in the United States and nationwide, shocking moments during the half-time show. Justin and Jackson sang Jackson's "All For You," "Rhythm

Nation," and Justin's "Rock Your Baby." Justin learned the night before that he would pull off part of Jackson's clothes to reveal a red top underneath when the last line of the song, "I gotta have you naked by the end of this song," was sung.

Unfortunately, when the time came, Justin accidentally pulled off more than he was supposed to and revealed Jackson's breast to all those watching both in the stadium and those watching on television. Almost immediately, complaints were being heard by the network and the Federal Communications Commission (FCC). More than 200,000 complaints came in over what was now dubbed as "Nipplegate."[9] Technology gave people the opportunity to view the incident over and over again on the Internet, on the news, and on sports shows. Chairman of

Singer Janet Jackson, left, covers her breast after her outfit came undone during a number with Justin Timberlake during the halftime show of Super Bowl XXXVIII in Houston, February 1, 2004. (AP Photo/Elise Amendola, File.)

the FCC, Michael Powell, was flabbergasted and ordered a full investigation into the incident: "I am outraged at what I saw. Like millions of Americans, my family and I gathered around the television for a celebration. Instead, that celebration was tainted by a classless, crass, and deplorable stunt. I have instructed the commission to open an immediate investigation into the broadcast. It will be thorough and swift."[10]

Justin coined the term *wardrobe malfunction* when he apologized after the incident. The phrase was continually used in the media to the point that it became a household word. The term was placed in the *Chambers English Dictionary* in its 2008 publication. The phrase is defined as "the temporary failure of an item of clothing to cover a part of the body that it would be advisable to keep covered." Other terms that were entered were social networking and nail bars. According to editor-in-chief Mary O'Neill, "The new words paint a vivid picture of current interests."[11]

Tony Perkins, head of the Family Research Council, a religious advocacy group, commented on the half-time show, "It's a sad day when parents can't even let their children watch the Super Bowl without having to worry about nudity creeping into their living rooms."[12] He was referring not only to Justin and Jackson but also Kid Rock's suggestive lyrics and Nelly's crotch grabbing. Executives said it would be unlikely that MTV would produce the Super Bowl half-time show again.

The repercussions from Nipplegate included a fine against CBS from the FCC in the amount of $550,000. The FCC called the accident indecent. The NFL also announced that MTV would never be commissioned to do another half-time show. CBS contested the network's fine because the incident was "unintentional and thus exempt from indecency regulation."[13] According to the *New York Times*, "In July 2008, the United States Court of Appeals for the Third Circuit voided the FCC's fine, but in May 2009 the Supreme Court vacated that judgment and sent the case back to the Third Circuit for reconsideration."[14] In 2009 the incident was listed in *Entertainment Weekly's* "10 Biggest Celebrity Scandals of the Decade." It topped the list with Britney Spears' meltdown; Winona Ryder's arrest for shoplifting at Saks; R. Kelly acquitted of pornography charges; Brad Pitt and his divorce from Jennifer Aniston and relationship with Angelina Jolie; Mel Gibson's DUI and anti-Semitic comments; Isaiah Washington's termination on *Grey's*

Anatomy for allegedly referring to costar T. R. Knight as a faggot on the set; Christian Bale's profanity-filled rant on the set of the *Terminator Salvation* film, which was leaked on the Internet; Jon and Kate Gosselin's announcement of their divorce on their reality show *Jon and Kate Plus* 8; and the assault of Rihanna by then-boyfriend Chris Brown.

Many viewers believed the "costume reveal" or "wardrobe malfunction" infringed on their rights to expect a decent Super Bowl. Civil lawsuits against Jackson and Justin erupted and were eventually dropped or dismissed because the FCC was already investigating the incident. "CBS contended the broadcast itself could not be considered explicit or graphic and that the FCC, in punishing the network, had abandoned its previous position that 'fleeting, isolated or unintended' scenes should not be regarded as indecent," according to an article on the Studio Briefing Film News web site.[15] AOL wanted the $7.5 million returned that it gave to the network to sponsor and advertise during the half-time show. The CBS network did issue a public apology for the antics during the half-time show.

Jackson and Justin were instructed to apologize to the public or forgo the Grammys, which they were to attend later in the month. Author Kathleen Tracey stated, "As a result of the controversy, the National Academy of Recording Arts & Sciences (NARAS), which sponsors the Grammys, announced that Timberlake and Jackson would be banned from the Grammy Award ceremony being held that week unless they apologized on the air."[16] A five-minute audio and visual delay was added to the aired CBS broadcast to avoid any further problems. In the aftermath, Jackson withdrew from the Grammys and made an official public apology. In the statement, she acknowledged that the reveal was her idea but that it was only supposed to reveal her red clothes underneath. Accompanied by his mother, Justin apologized both before and during the Grammys. His comment at the telecast when he accepted a Grammy for Best Male Pop Vocal Performance for *Justified* was, "What occurred was unintentional, completely regrettable, and I apologize if you guys are offended."[17] Justin went on to perform at the event with jazz personality Arturo Sandoval. His $6 million contract for the McDonald's "I'm Lovin' It" campaign was saved despite the controversy after Justin publicly apologized and said the incident had been an unfortunate mistake for all involved.

Justin Timberlake holds the awards he won for best male pop vocal performance and best pop vocal album at the 46th Annual Grammy Awards, February 8, 2004, in Los Angeles. (AP Photo/Mark J. Terrill.)

Justin was also slated to cohost a *Motown 45* television special with Lionel Ritchie. Other musicians scheduled for the show included Mary J. Blige, the Temptations, and the Four Tops. ABC network executives said that Justin had pulled out of the special because of other acting commitments, not because of protests from African American groups. In an article from Reuters, the Project Islamic HOPE group prepared a statement that read, "The selection of Timberlake as cohost of the Motown special is a cultural insult to the black community. This special, celebrating the success of the legendary music label, should not be compromised in the pursuit of a crossover audience."[18] Justin had also never recorded with the label that was sponsoring the show so protestors were uncertain why he was even slated as one of the hosts of the show. The members "felt that he let Janet Jackson take the full blame for her flesh-baring stunt."[19] He was to start filming *Edison* with Kevin Spacey and Morgan Freeman in Canada at the same time as the television special.

After the Super Bowl half-time fiasco, both Justin and Jackson had many public relations issues. The pinnacle of the situation was when Tennessee banker Terri Carlin filed a lawsuit against Justin, Jackson, CBS, MTV, and Viacom on behalf of all Americans. The papers, filed in the U.S. District Court, stated that the show caused her "outrage, anger, embarrassment, and serious injury."[20] The suit was asking for millions of dollars in compensatory and punitive damages for all American people. The suit caused hundreds of fans to email and call both Carlin and her attorney Wayne A. Ritchie II to voice their displeasure over the legal action against the pop stars. The suit was eventually dismissed. Three months later, a Farmington Utah lawyer, filed a lawsuit against Viacom. Eric Stephenson tried to make a claim that the Super Bowl half-time show was falsely advertised in television commercials leading up to the show. Based on the pregame advertising he thought the half-time show would consist of marching bands and balloons. His suit was rejected because he did not go through proper channels and file a complaint with the FCC or put together a federal lawsuit, according to an Associated Press article.[21]

The Super Bowl half-time show also affected Justin's friend JC Chasez. Chasez was to perform at the half-time show at the Pro Bowl on February 8, 2004. He was supposed to sing the National Anthem to begin the game and his song, "Blowin' Me Up (With Her Love)" at half-time. His was unable to perform during the half-time show because of the sexual content of his song. He was replaced by traditional Hawaiian dancers because the Pro Bowl took place in Hawaii. Amidst the controversy many award shows, soap operas, and prime-time shows took the time to clean up their shows before they aired instead of facing penalties by the FCC. Victoria Secret's annual fashion show was also postponed indefinitely for 2004.

After the Super Bowl controversy Justin had thoughts of putting his music career on hold to pursue an acting career. He tried to deal with the media during the situation by just ignoring them and telling them what happened and what was supposed to happen. Often in the media, people's minds were made up to what they thought happened. "Sometimes you just want your life to be your life, not everybody else's to speculate on. As far as the press is concerned, they're going to say what they want to say . . . Probably about ten to fifteen percent of the time it's accurate," Justin commented.[22]

Justin's troubles continued in 2004 with a situation in November involving the paparazzi. Outside the Chateau Marmont Hotel in Hollywood with Cameron Diaz, Justin allegedly became fed up with the media and slapped one of two men, journalists Saul Lazo and Jose Gonzalez. The paparazzi sued the celebrities claiming emotional distress and physical harm. The district attorney in the case reprimanded Justin saying he should not retaliate against the paparazzi with violence. The celebrities countersued the photographers, alleging that they were attacked by them when they were trying to have a quiet night out. Diaz stole one the cameras. In court papers she said she took the camera "for purposes of later trying to identify the men."[23] After the incident both Diaz and Justin stated that they were acting in self defense. The two sides settled the case with an undisclosed settlement, according to a World Entertainment News Network article.[24]

Justin's court woes did not stop with the paparazzi. He filed charges against the British newspaper *News of the World* in August 2005. The newspaper published a false report that Justin was having relations with model Lucy Clarkson. London's High Court found in favor of Justin. Clarkson was told to give Justin the money she had received for the story. He in turn donated the money to charity. According to a 2005 World Entertainment News Network article, the story had run during Justin's relationship with Cameron Diaz.[25] A few months after Justin won his libel case, Diaz filed charges against another British newspaper, *The Sun*, that had run the story that Diaz had an affair with Shane Nickerson, an MTV producer, and published a picture of the two of them hugging. Diaz was dating Justin at the time and Nickerson is married to Elisa and has a daughter named Lucy. The newspaper paid Diaz's legal fees and ran an apology in the newspaper. She also sued the *National Enquirer* for a $30 million claim earlier in the year for the same story about her having an alleged affair with Nickerson. Nickerson and Diaz were working together on the MTV show *Trippin'*. "The suit claims the published story has not only damaged both of their reputations, but also placed needless strains on their personal relationships," reported *USA Today*.[26]

Because of Justin's success, many media and critics ask him about the up-and-coming singers and what he thinks about them. In 2006 when he was asked about *American Idol* winner Taylor Hicks, he told *Fashion*

Actress Cameron Diaz, left, and Justin Timberlake chat as they watch other participants warm up before a children's charity basketball game hosted by 'NSync on July 25, 2004, in Sunrise, Florida. (AP Photo/Wilfredo Lee.)

Rocks magazine that Hicks could not "carry a tune in a bucket."[27] Justin's publicist Ken Sunshine told the media that the comments Justin made about Hicks were taken out of context and he has nothing but well wishes for the rising music star. Justin continued the interview hinting that Hicks may not have a long singing career, commenting, "If he has any skeletons whatsoever—if, God forbid, he was gay—and all these people in Mississippi who voted for him are like, 'Oh, my God, I voted for a queer!' It's just too much pressure."[28]

Southern Hospitality, a restaurant in New York that Justin is affiliated with, has been sued twice by former employees. In November 2008, a busboy, Felipe Ramales, claimed that he was not being paid for overtime or for tips to which he was entitled. Chris Russell, the manager at the restaurant, said the lawsuit was false and "staff members received every dime of their tips, and busboys were paid well over minimum wage."[29] In another suit against the restaurant, former manager and aspiring actress, Alison McDaniel, filed a sexual discrimination lawsuit. She claims that in her job she was "spit on, pelted with expletives and subjected to porn."[30] Justin, Trace Ayala, Eytan Sugarman, Ronnie Kaplan, and the restaurant are named as defendants. McDaniel was let go after her lawsuit was filed but she did not file a complaint with the Equal Opportunity Employment Commission.

Being a celebrity also brings with it people who think they are in love with you and adore you, but in reality, they don't know you and will probably never even get the chance to meet that celebrity. Justin had once such an occurrence with a stalker. On October 22, 2009, 48-year-old Karen J. McNeil arrived at Justin's Los Angeles home in a cab with her belongings. McNeil represented herself in court and testified that she was destined to marry Justin. In October 2009, Justin received a restraining order against alleged stalker McNeil. The restraining order is a permanent restraining order meaning it is in place for three years. Court documents state that McNeil had trespassed on the Timberlake property more than three times and she could be homeless. Documents state that McNeil's actions have "become much more alarming and her motivation and obsession have become more ominous, intrusive and threatening."[31] Justin also said in court documents that he is afraid for his safety. The restraining order states that McNeil must stay 100 yards away from Justin and his property.

Fans become obsessed with celebrities and try to obtain everything they can to feel close to the famous person. In spring 2000, Justin's French toast was sold on EBay for $1,025. After Justin didn't finish his breakfast at an interview with Z-100 in New York, the DJ put the uneaten French toast on the Internet retail site. Kathy Summers, a 19-year-old from Madison, Wisconsin, was the highest bidder. She freeze-dried it, sealed it up, and displayed it proudly as belonging to Justin Timberlake.

In a lawsuit filed in November 2009, Justin is named as a defendant, with the L.A. Lakers, Britney Spears, and the Pussycat Dolls. The suit alleges that the four used the Jumbo Tron TV in their concerts and performances without permission. Large Audience Display Systems LLC holds the patent for the Jumbo Tron TV and did not give the performers a license to use their equipment in the shows. Justin used the equipment in his *FutureSex/LoveShow* Tour. The entertainers are specifically being sued for patent infringement, according to a TMZ Celebrity article.[32]

Despite Justin's successes, as a celebrity there will always be scrutiny, criticism, and obstacles to overcome. Justin has taken on his obstacles with grace, realizing that when he disappoints his fans he needs to get back in their graces because they are what made him a success.

NOTES

1. Clark Collis, "Sexy Beat," *Entertainment Weekly*, February 9, 2007, p. 36.

2. Sean Smith, *Justin: The Unauthorized Biography* (New York: Pocket Books, 2004), p. 127.

3. Smith, *Justin*, p. 129.

4. Joseph Patel, "'NSync Members Accused of Being Racists in Suit by Former Tour Manager," *MTV News*, December 17, 2003, http://www.mtvnews.com.

5. "Timberlake in Racist Slur Accusation," *ContactMusic.com*, December 15, 2003.

6. Stephen M. Silverman, "Justin Timberlake: The Hoax 'Sucks,'" *People*, June 22, 2001.

7. "Djs Fired After Starting Spears-Timberlake Hoax," *Hollywood.com*, June 20, 2001.

8. "Janet Convinced Justin to Perform at Super Bowl," *ContactMusic.com*, February 5, 2004.

9. Kathleen Tracey, *Justin Timberlake: Blue Banner Biography* (Hockessin, DE: Mitchell Lane Publishers, 2008), p. 7.

10. "Jackson Admits Super Bowl Stunt Was Intentional," *World Entertainment News Network*, February 4, 2004.

11. Daniel Kilkelly, "'Wardrobe Malfunction' Enters Dictionary," *Digital Spy*, August 14, 2008.

12. "Nipplegate," *Studio Briefing Film News*, February 3, 2004.

13. "Viacom to Pay Record $3.5 Million to Settle FCC Indecency Cases," *Online NewsHour*, November 24, 2004.

14. "Justices Tell Appeals Court to Revisit Super Bowl Incident," *New York Times*, May 4, 2009.

15. "CBS Defends Janet Jackson Telecast," *Studio Briefing Film News*, November 21, 2006.

16. Tracey, *Justin Timberlake*, p. 7.

17. "Timberlake Sings 'I Apologize'—Jackson Doesn't," *Studio Briefing Film News*, February 9, 2009.

18. Todd Peterson, "Justin Timberlake: A Motown No-Show," *People*, February 25, 2004.

19. Jennifer Vineyard, "Timberlake Pulls Out of Motown Special in Wake of Protests," *MTV News*, February 25, 2004.

20. "Banker Withdraws Jackson and Timberlake Lawsuit," *World Entertainment News Network*, February 11, 2004.

21. "Judge Rules against Super Bowl Viewer," Associated Press, May 27, 2005.

22. Tracey, *Justin Timberlake*, p. 23.

23. "Diaz Fights Back," *World Entertainment News Network*, December 27, 2004.

24. "Timberlake and Diaz Settle with Photographers," *World Entertainment News Network*, June 10, 2005.

25. "Timberlake Accepts Libel Damages," *World Entertainment News Network*, August 25, 2005.

26. "Cameron Diaz Sues *The National Enquirer*," *USA Today*, June 3, 2005.

27. "Justin Timberlake: Taylor Hicks 'Can't Carry a Tune in a Bucket,'" Associated Press, August 17, 2006.

28. Stephen M. Silverman, "Justin: Taylor Hicks 'Can't Carry a Tune in a Bucket,'" *People*, August 17, 2006.

29. "Justin Timberlake Sued by Restaurant Employee," *X17 Online News*, November 17, 2008.

30. Melissa Grace, "Justin Timberlake's Southern Hospitality Restaurant Slapped with Sexual Discrimination Lawsuit," *New York Daily News*, May 15, 2009.

31. "Justin Timberlake Gets Restraining Order against Karen J. McNeil," *Huffington Post*, October 23, 2009.

32. "Britney, Justin, Lakers Sued," *TMZ Celeb*, November 13, 2009.

CHAPTER 9

"UNTIL THE END OF TIME"

Justin's career as a musician and entertainer has been an ongoing mission of his life since his very early teens. His fortunate success as a Mouseketeer and as the lead singer of a boy band has led him to pursue other opportunities, such as acting, producing, and business ownership with confidence.

The endurance of a celebrity includes giving up a great deal of privacy in your life and having the paparazzi constantly pursuing stories and snapshots. This is one of those elements that Justin sees as a sacrifice he is willing to make for his dreams to come true: "If you want to do something that you love to do, you make sacrifices to do it. And that's what I have done. Everyone always asks 'Do you regret missing your teenage years?' But I haven't missed anything. I've gained so much more that a lot of people can't have. I don't regret anything, because this is what I love to do, and I am happy that I found this out at such an early age."[1]

Throughout his career, Justin's family has been a constant bevy of support for anything that he pursues. His mother Lynn told him at an early age not to do "half-ass" things.[2] She has been Justin's constant traveling companion since he moved to Orlando to do *The All-New Mickey Mouse Club* and 'NSync.

Despite his enormous success as a musician, actor, entrepreneur, and producer, Justin realizes his role in impacting where he came from and where he is now by establishing music foundations, appearing at benefits, and hosting awards shows. As many celebrities before him, Justin realizes that to keep his fan base he must retain a positive image in the media spotlight. His home state of Tennessee has been given a lot through Justin's philanthropy and humanitarianism.

To date, Justin has composed 93 songs that are listed with the American Society of Composers, Authors, and Publishers (ASCAP).[3] This is an achievement that has been in the making for more than a decade when Justin first became a member of 'NSync. Many musicians emulate Justin and respect him for his musical genius. Kanye West, a rapper, sees Justin as his musical equivalent. In an interview with *American XXL* magazine, West said, "My biggest inspiration and biggest competition is Justin Timberlake. He's the only person that gets an across-the-board response and respect level—black radio, white radio. If Justin hadn't come out and killed the game, I can't say that my album, singles and videos would be on the same level that they're on. We push each other. I look at me and Justin like Prince and Michael Jackson in their day."[4]

Aside from having a long list of accomplishments to his name already, Justin too has dreams of continuing on in the rock and roll industry. He also sees himself slowing down a bit to pursue other interests: "The dream is to be able to have a schedule like I've had the last five years, to put out a record and tour, then take a little break, maybe do some films. But I don't want to work this hard forever."[5]

For any celebrity to be successful in his field, he needs to build relationships with his fans and with people in the industry. Justin has successfully reached the top of the music industry. He has done this through determination and taking risks. His career is far from over as he continues to write and produce music. Justin's philosophy has been to work hard to achieve whatever it is you want to do in life: "Regardless of whether you want to be a singer, doctor or lawyer, learn all you can about it. Then if you give 150 percent, you'll get a 100 percent outcome."[6]

NOTES

1. Kathleen Tracey, *Justin Timberlake: Blue Banner Biography* (Hockessin, DE: Mitchell Lane Publishers, 2008), p. 16.

2. Adam Rapport, "The 10 Most Stylish Men in America," *Gentlemen's Quarterly*, March 2009, p. 178.

3. Holly Cefrey, *Justin Timberlake: Contemporary Musicians and Their Music* (New York: Rosen Publishing, 2009), p. 31.

4. "West Pays Tribute to Timberlake Inspiration," *World Entertainment News Network*, August 22, 2007, http://femalefirst.co.uk/music/musicnews/Kanye+West-39401.html.

5. Terri Dougherty, *Justin Timberlake: People in the News* (Farmington Hills, MI: Lucent Books, 2008), p. 87.

6. Tracey, *Justin Timberlake*, p. 27.

APPENDICES

DISCOGRAPHY

'NSYNC ALBUMS

*NSYNC (released May 26, 1997, by BMG Munich, Germany; released March 24, 1998, by RCA Records in the United States)

1. "Tearin' Up My Heart"
2. "I Just Wanna Be with You"
3. "Here We Go"
4. "For the Girl Who Has Everything"
5. "God Must Have Spent a Little More Time on You"
6. "You Got It"
7. "I Need Love"
8. "I Want You Back"
9. "Everything I Own"
10. "I Drive Myself Crazy"
11. "Crazy for You"
12. "Sailing"
13. "Giddy Up"

Home for Christmas (released November 10, 1998, by RCA Records)

1. "Home for Christmas"
2. "Under My Tree"
3. "I Never Knew the Meaning of Christmas"
4. "Merry Christmas, Happy Holidays"
5. "The Christmas Song (Chestnuts Roasting on an Open Fire)"
6. "I Guess It's Christmas Time"
7. "All I Want Is You This Christmas"
8. "The First Noel"
9. "In Love on Christmas"
10. "It's Christmas"
11. "O Holy Night" (A Cappella)
12. "Love's in Our Hearts on Christmas Day"
13. "The Only Gift"

The Winter Album (released November 17, 1998, by BMG International in Europe)

1. "U Drive Me Crazy" (Radio Edit)
2. "God Must Have Spent a Little More Time on You"
3. "Thinking of You"
4. "Everything I Own"
5. "I Just Wanna Be with You"
6. "Kiss Me at Midnight"
7. "Merry Christmas, Happy Holidays"
8. "All I Want Is You This Christmas"
9. "Under My Tree"
10. "Love's in Our Hearts on Christmas Day"
11. "In Love on Christmas"
12. "The First Noel"

No Strings Attached (released March 21, 2000, by Jive Records)

1. "Bye Bye Bye"
2. "It's Gonna Be Me"
3. "Space Cowboy"
4. "Just Got Paid"

5. "It Makes Me Ill"
6. "This I Promise You"
7. "No Strings Attached"
8. "Digital Getdown"
9. "Bringin' Da Noise"
10. "That's When I'll Stop Loving You"
11. "I'll Be Good for You"
12. "I Thought She Knew"

Celebrity (released July 24, 2001, by Jive Records)

1. "Pop"
2. "Celebrity"
3. "The Game Is Over"
4. "Girlfriend"
5. "The Two of Us"
6. "Gone"
7. "Tell Me, Tell Me . . . Baby"
8. "Up against the Wall"
9. "See Right through You"
10. "Selfish"
11. "Don't Tell Me That"
12. "Something Like You"
13. "Do Your Thing"

Greatest Hits (released October 25, 2005, by Jive Records)

1. "Bye Bye Bye"
2. "Girlfriend" (with Nelly)
3. "This I Promise You"
4. "It's Gonna Be Me"
5. "God Must Have Spent a Little More Time on You"
6. "I Want You Back"
7. "Pop"
8. "Gone"
9. "Tearin' Up My Heart"
10. "I Drove Myself Crazy"
11. "I'll Never Stop"
12. "Music of My Heart" (with Gloria Estefan)

JUSTIN TIMBERLAKE SOLO ALBUMS

Justified (released November 5, 2002, by Jive Records)

1. "Señorita"
2. "(Oh No) What You Got"
3. "Take It from Here"
4. "Cry Me a River"
5. "Rock Your Body"
6. "Nothin' Else"
7. "Like I Love You"
8. "Still on My Brain"
9. "(And She Said) Take Me Now"
10. "Right for Me"
11. "Let's Take a Ride"
12. "Never Again"

FutureSex/LoveSounds (released September 12, 2006, by Jive Records)

1. "FutureSex/LoveSounds"
2. "SexyBack" (with Timbaland)
3. "Sexy Ladies/Let Me Talk to You" Prelude
4. "My Love" (with T. I.)
5. "Love Stoned/I Think She Knows" Interlude
6. "What Goes Around . . . / . . . Comes Around" Interlude
7. "Chop Me Up" (with Three 6 Mafia and Timbaland)
8. "Damn Girl" (with will.i.am)
9. "Summer Love/Set the Mood" Prelude
10. "Until the End of Time" (with Benjamin Orchestra Wright)
11. "Losing My Way"
12. "(Another Song) All Over Again"

COLLABORATIONS

"Work It" (with Nelly), 2002
"Where Is the Love?" (with Black Eyed Peas), 2003
"Signs" (with Snoop Dogg), 2005
"Give It to Me" (with Nelly Furtado and Timbaland), 2007

"Ayo Technology" (with 50 Cent and Timbaland), 2007

"Falling Down" (with Duran Duran), 2007

"Nite Runner" (with Duran Duran and Timbaland), 2007

"The Only Promise That Remains" (with Reba McEntire), 2007

"4 Minutes" (with Madonna), 2007

"Rehab" (with Rihanna), 2008

"Don't Let Me Down" (with Leona Lewis), 2009

Singles

"Steppin' Out Tonight," 2008

"Magic," 2008

FILMOGRAPHY

FILM

Yogi Bear, released December 17, 2010, by Warner Brothers
Directed by Eric Brevig, this animated film takes place in Jelly Stone Park. Justin does the voice-over for Boo-Boo Bear, Yogi Bear's sidekick. The Mayor has been using money from the city for his own personal use, so Jelly Stone Park is going bankrupt. To recoup the money, the Mayor wants to sell Jelly Stone Park. Yogi and Boo-Boo join with Ranger Smith to save the park. A documentary filmmaker has come to shoot a project in the park and becomes involved in Yogi and Boo-Boo's antics. Dan Aykroyd, Anna Faris, Andy Daly, and Tom Cavanagh also join the cast.

The Social Network, released October 15, 2010, by Columbia Pictures
Based on the founding of the international social site Facebook, this film relates the rise to wealth, fame, and power of the founders. Written by Aaron Sorkin and directed by David Fincher, the film concentrates on Mark Zuckerberg and his roommates who built the social network while they were sophomores at Harvard. Justin plays Sean Parker, the president of Napster who became one of the founders of Facebook. Other stars in the film include Jesse Eisenberg, Andrew Garfield, and Rashida Jones.

Shrek Forever After, released May 21, 2010, by DreamWorks Paramount
Pictures

In this animated film, Justin reprises his voice-over role as Prince Artie.
Shrek signs a pact with Rumplestiltskin, everything reverts back to the
past, and Shrek and Fiona have never met. The film has a similar plot
to the movie *Far, Far Away*. Shrek has to undo everything that he did
to make sure that his world is restored and he is reunited with his one
true love. Justin is cast again with Mike Myers, Cameron Diaz, Eddie
Murphy, and Antonio Banderas.

The Open Road, released August 28, 2009, by Anchor Bay Entertainment,
Heavy Lifting, and Odd Lot Entertainment

Justin portrays Carlton Garrett, a baseball player who has to find his
estranged father after his mother takes ill and requests her ex-husband's
presence at her bedside. Together with his girlfriend, the two take to
the road to find his father at a baseball-card convention and journey
home. The moral of the story is that it is about the journey, not the
destination. Jeff Bridges plays Justin's father, Kyle, while veteran actress
Mary Steenburgen plays Justin's mother. Others in the cast include Kate
Mara, Harry Dean Stanton, Ted Danson, and Lyle Lovett.

The Love Guru, released June 20, 2008, by Paramount Pictures Spyglass
Entertainment

A comedy, written by Mike Meyers and Graham Gordy, *The Love Guru*
takes the sport of hockey to a new level. Pitka, the guru, must help
Toronto Maple Leaf player Darren Roanoke improve his game and
win back the affections of his wife who has fallen in love with another
hockey player. Justin plays Jacques Grande, the Kings player whom the
wife falls in love with.

Southland Tales, released November 14, 2007, by Samuel Goldwyn Films

Written by Richard Kelly, this film depicts a terrorist attack on the
United States. Justin plays Private Pilot Abilene who is an Iraqi war vet
who narrates the story. Videotaped footage of July 4, 2005, begins the
film and shows a nuclear attack on Abilene, Texas. Two nuclear weapons were unleashed on Texas, and World War III is now being fought
between Iraq, Afghanistan, Syria, and Korea. With an oil crisis now in
Texas, government agencies try to find a solution. The film debuted at
the Cannes Film Festival to mixed reviews. After the festival, the movie
was revamped to include more special effects.

Shrek the Third, released May 18, 2007, by DreamWorks Paramount Pictures
Justin is the voice of Prince Artie. After the king dies, Shrek does not want to be king, so he goes on a quest to find the real heir to the throne, Prince Artie. Ultimately, Shrek wants to return to his swamp with his pregnant Fiona. While on his quest, Prince Charming comes in to try and take over the kingdom, so when Artie and Shrek return from their journey, they must fight off the villainous Prince Charming. Justin made a cameo as a poster of Prince Justin in Shrek II when his picture was seen on the wall of Princess Fiona's bedroom. Other returning cast members include Mike Meyers, Eddie Murphy, Cameron Diaz, Antonio Banderas, and Rupert Everett.

Black Snake Moan, released March 2, 2007, by Paramount Vantage
In this drama, Justin finds himself playing Ronnie, a misguided youth who has been discharged from the army due to anxiety issues. Rae, played by Christina Ricci, is a teenager who is verbally and sexually abused by her parents. When she is left for dead, she is found by Lazarus, portrayed by Samuel L. Jackson, whose wife has just left him. Lazarus takes Rae under his wing to nurse her back to health and give her some fatherly advice. When Ronnie comes back from the service, he misinterprets the relationship between his girlfriend and her mentor and vows to kill Lazarus. Lazarus tries to help the two find their way in life.

Alpha Dog, released January 12, 2007, by Universal Pictures
Based on a true case, *Alpha Dog*, is a drama about the kidnap and murder of a 15-year-old boy whose older brother owed drug money. Justin plays Frankie Ballenbacher, one of the gangsters who kidnaps Zack Mazursky. Although Zack is brought into the life of the drug dealers and attends parties, he is uncertain of his true role of being kidnapped. Zack turns up dead at the hand of the gangsters and their leader, Johnny Truelove, for fear that Zack may talk if they let him go. Although Frankie is caught and sentenced to prison, Johnny flees to Paraguay and is not captured until five years after the crime occurred. This highly controversial film also stars Bruce Willis, Emile Hirsch, Vincent Kartheiser, and Shawn Hatosy.

Edison Force, released July 18, 2006, by Brightlight Pictures
This straight-to-video film is a crime drama about a young journalist who uncovers corruption in the justice system when he is investigating a homicide case. Justin plays Josh Pollack, the young journalist on his

quest for truth. When finding injustices in the system, Pollack and his girlfriend become targets of those that don't want the truth to come to light. Pollack goes to his editor and veteran reporter for help. Although the film includes stars such as Morgan Freeman, Kevin Spacey, Dylan McDermott, and John Heard, it received bad reviews at many of the film festivals.

Longshot, released March 26, 2002, by PearlCam Productions
Also known as *Jack of All Trades* in the United States, this film centers around Jack Taylor, a Beverly Hills gigolo who is being blackmailed by a powerful businessman. He has to seduce a lovely businesswoman to get insider trading information but eventually falls in love with her. Justin only plays a bit part as a valet alongside his best friend Trace Ayala. JC Chasez, Joey Fatone, Chris Kirkpatrick, and Lance Bass also appear in the film.

TELEVISION

Elton John: The Red Piano, 2005
Justin plays the young Elton John in this commentary about Elton John's life.

Saturday Night Live, 2002–2009
Justin has hosted and been the musical guest on *Saturday Night Live* many times, beginning in 2002. He made famous two skits with Andy Samberg, including "Dick in a Box" and "Motherlover." The two comedy sketches have been on YouTube and have been accessed several times. In 2009, Justin became the first *Saturday Night Live* host to receive an Emmy.

Model Behavior, 2000
This Disney Channel made-for-TV movie is about two high school students who trade places because one wants to lead a normal life (because she is a model) and the other wishes for a glamorous life. Justin plays Jason Sharp, a young, good-looking model who dates one of the high school teens to further his own modeling career. This film is based on the book *Alex, Alex and Janine* by Michael Levin.

Touched by an Angel, 1999
Justin played a street performer in the episode titled "Voice of an Angel."

TELEVISION SHOW CREDITS AS HIMSELF

Punk'd: three episodes between 2003 and 2007

The Simpsons: "New Kids on the Blecch," 2001

Sesame Street: "Elmo in Numberland," 2000

Clueless: "None for the Road," 1999

Sabrina, the Teenage Witch: "Sabrina and the Pirates," 1999

The All-New Mickey Mouse Club: four episodes between 1993 and 1995

AWARDS AND NOMINATIONS

MUSICIAN WITH 'NSYNC

2003	Grammy Award Nomination	Best Pop Performance by a Duo or Group with Vocals for "Girlfriend"
2002	American Music Award	Favorite Pop/Rock Band/Duo/Group
2002	American Music Award Nomination	Favorite Pop/Rock Album for *Celebrity*
2002	Grammy Award Nomination	Best Pop Performance by a Duo or Group with Vocals for "Gone"
2002	Grammy Award Nomination	Best Pop Vocal Album for *Celebrity*
2002	MTV Video Music Award Nomination	Video of the Year for "Gone"
2002	MTV Video Music Award Nomination	Best Group Video
2002	MTV Video Music Award Nomination	Best Pop Video for "Girlfriend" (remix) with Nelly

2002	People's Choice Award	Favorite Musical Group or Band
2002	Teen Choice Award	Choice Hook Up for "Girlfriend" with Nelly
2002	Teen Choice Award Nomination	Choice Single for "Girlfriend" with Nelly
2001	American Music Award	Internet Fans Artist of the Year Award
2001	American Music Award Nomination	Favorite Pop/Rock Band/Duo/Group
2001	American Music Award Nomination	Favorite Pop/Rock Album for *No Strings Attached*
2001	Blockbuster Award	Favorite CD
2001	Blockbuster Award	Favorite Group—Pop
2001	Blockbuster Award	Favorite Single for "Bye Bye Bye"
2001	Blockbuster Award Nomination	Favorite Group
2001	Grammy Award Nomination	Record of the Year for "Bye Bye Bye"
2001	Grammy Award Nomination	Best Pop Performance by a Duo or Group with Vocals for "Bye Bye Bye"
2001	Grammy Award Nomination	Best Pop Vocal Album for *No Strings Attached*
2001	Juno Award Nomination	Best Selling Album for *No Strings Attached*
2001	Kids' Choice Award	Favorite Song for "Bye Bye Bye"
2001	Kids' Choice Award	Favorite Singing Group
2001	MTV Europe Music Award Nomination	Best Pop Act
2001	MTV Video Music Award	Best Group Video for "Pop"
2001	MTV Video Music Award	Best Pop Video for "Pop"
2001	MTV Video Music Award	Best Dance Video for "Pop"
2001	MTV Video Music Award	Viewer's Choice for "Pop"

2001	MTV Video Music Award Nomination	Breakthrough Video for "Pop"
2001	People's Choice Award	Favorite Musical Group or Band
2001	Teen Choice Award	Choice Single for "Pop"
2001	Teen Choice Award	Choice Album for *Celebrity*
2001	Teen Choice Award	Choice Concert
2000	Blockbuster Award	Favorite Song from a Movie for "Music of My Heart"
2000	Grammy Award Nomination	Best Pop Collaboration with Vocals for "Music of My Heart" with Gloria Estefan
2000	Grammy Award Nomination	Best Country Collaboration with Vocals for "God Must Have Spent a Little More Time on You" with Alabama
2000	MuchMovie Video Music Award	Favorite International Group for "Bye Bye Bye"
2000	MuchMovie Video Music Award Nomination	Best International Video for "Bye Bye Bye"
2000	Radio Music Award	Song of the Year: Top 40/Pop Radio for "Bye Bye Bye"
2000	Radio Music Award	Artist of the Year: Top 40/Pop Radio
2000	Teen Choice Award	Choice Pop Group
2000	Teen Choice Award	Song of the Summer for "Bye Bye Bye"
2000	Teen Choice Award	Choice Music Video for "Bye Bye Bye"
2000	Teen Choice Award	Choice Single for "Bye Bye Bye"
2000	Academy of Country Music Nomination	Top Vocal Event of the Year for "God Must Have Spent a Little More Time on You"

2000	American Music Award Nomination	Favorite Band/Duo/Group
2000	Kids' Choice Award Nomination	Favorite Song from a Movie "Music of My Heart"
2000	Kids' Choice Award Nomination	Favorite Musical Group
2000	MTV Video Music Award	Best Pop Video for "Bye Bye Bye"
2000	MTV Video Music Award	Viewer's Choice for "Bye Bye Bye"
2000	MTV Video Music Award Nomination	Video of the Year for "Bye Bye Bye"
2000	MTV Video Music Award Nomination	Best Group Video for "Bye Bye Bye"
2000	MTV Video Music Award Nomination	Best Dance Video for "Bye Bye Bye"
1999	Academy of Country Music	Best Pop New Artist Award
1999	Teen Choice Award	Album of the Year for *NSYNC
1999	MTV Video Music Award Nomination	Best Group Video for "Tearin' Up My Heart"
1999	MTV Video Music Award Nomination	Best New Artist Video for "Tearin' Up My Heart"
1999	MTV Video Music Award Nomination	Best Pop Video for "Tearin' Up My Heart"
1999	MTV Video Music Award Nomination	Viewer's Choice for "Tearin' Up My Heart"
1999	Blockbuster Award	Favorite New Artist—Group
1998	Billboard Video Music Award	Best Clip for "I Want You Back"
1998	Billboard Video Music Award	Best New Artist Clip for "I Want You Back"
1998	Billboard Video Music Award Nomination	Best New Artist for "Tearin' Up My Heart"

SOLO CAREER

2009	Grammy Award Nomination	Best Collaboration with Vocals for "4 Minutes" with Madonna and Timbaland
2009	Grammy Award Nomination	Best Remixed Recording for "4 Minutes" with Madonna and Timbaland
2008	Grammy Award Nomination	Record of the Year for "What Goes Around . . . / . . . Comes Around"
2008	Grammy Award	Best Male Pop Vocal Performance for "What Goes Around . . . / . . . Comes Around"
2008	Grammy Award	Best Dance Recording for "Lovestoned/I Think She Knows"
2008	Grammy Award Nomination	Best Pop Collaboration with Vocals for "Give It to Me" with Timbaland and Nelly Furtado
2008	Grammy Award Nomination	Best Rap Song for "Ayo Technology" with 50 Cent and Timbaland
2008	NRJ Award	Best International Male Artist
2008	MTV Video Music Award Nomination	Best Dancing in a Video for "4 Minutes" with Madonna
2007	World Music Award	World's Best Selling Pop Male Artist of the Year
2007	World Music Award	World's Best Selling American Artist of the Year
2007	MTV Video Music Award Nomination	Video of the Year for "What Goes Around . . . / . . . Comes Around"
2007	MTV Video Music Award	Male Artist of the Year

2007	MTV Video Music Award Nomination	Most Earth-Shattering Collaboration for "Sexy-Back" with Timbaland
2007	MTV Video Music Award	Quadruple Threat of the Year
2007	MTV Video Music Award	Best Direction for "What Goes Around . . . / . . . Comes Around"
2007	MTV Video Music Award	Best Choreography for "My Love" with T. I.
2007	MTV Video Music Award Nomination	Best Editing for "What Goes Around . . . / . . . Comes Around"
2007	Grammy Award	Best Male Pop Vocal Performance for "What Goes Around . . . / . . . Comes Around"
2007	Grammy Award	Best Dance Recording for "Lovestoned/I Think She Knows"
2007	American Music Award	Favorite Pop/Rock Male Artist
2007	American Music Award Nomination	Favorite Pop/Rock Album for *FutureSex/LoveSounds*
2007	American Music Award	Favorite R&B/Soul Album for *FutureSex/LoveSounds*
2007	BRIT Award	Best International Male Artist
2007	BRIT Award Nomination	Best International Album for *FutureSex/LoveSounds*
2006	Grammy Award	Best Dance Recording for "SexyBack"
2006	Grammy Award	Best Rap/Sung Collaboration for "My Love"
2006	Grammy Award Nomination	Best Pop Vocal Album for *FutureSex/LoveSounds*
2006	Grammy Award Nomination	Album of the Year for *FutureSex/LoveSounds*

2004	Grammy Award Nomination	Record of the Year for "Where Is the Love?" with the Black Eyed Peas
2004	Grammy Award Nomination	Best Rap/Sung Collaboration for "Where Is the Love?" with the Black Eyed Peas
2004	BRIT Award	Best International Album for *Justified*
2004	BRIT Award Nomination	Best Pop Act
2004	MTV Video Music Award Nomination	Best Male Video for "Señorita" with Pharrell
2004	BET Award Nomination	Sexiest Male Singer of the Year
2004	BRIT Award	Best International Male Artist
2004	Grammy Award	Best Pop Vocal Album for *Justified*
2004	Grammy Award	Best Male Pop Vocal Performance for "Cry Me a River"
2003	Soul Train Award Nomination	Best R&B/Soul Male Single for "Like I Love You" with the Clipse
2003	Soul Train Award Nomination	Best R&B/Soul Male Album for *Justified*
2003	Vibe Music Award Nomination	Album of the Year for *Justified*
2003	BET Award Nomination	Best R&B Male Artist
2003	BET Award Nomination	Best New Artist
2003	MTV Video Music Award	Best Male Video for "Cry Me a River" with Timbaland
2003	MTV Video Music Award	Best Pop Video for "Cry Me a River" with Timbaland
2003	MTV Video Music Award	Best Dance Video for "Rock Your Body"
2003	MTV Video Music Award Nomination	Viewer's Choice for "Cry Me a River" with Timbaland

2003	MTV Video Music Award Nomination	Best Direction for "Cry Me a River" with Timbaland
2003	MTV Video Music Award Nomination	Best Choreography for "Rock Your Body"
2003	American Music Award	Favorite Pop/Rock Album for *Justified*
2003	American Music Award Nomination	Favorite Pop/Rock Male Artist
2003	American Music Award Nomination	Fan Choice Award
2003	Grammy Award Nomination	Best Rap/Sung Collaboration for "Like I Love You" with the Clipse
2002	Grammy Award Nomination	Best Pop Collaboration with Vocals for "My Kind of Girl" with Brian McKnight

ACTOR

2009	Emmy Award	Outstanding Guest Actor in a Comedy Series for *Saturday Night Live*
2009	Emmy Nomination	Outstanding Original Music and Lyrics for *Saturday Night Live*; "Motherlover"
2009	Emmy Nomination	Outstanding Original Music and Lyrics for *ESPY Awards*; "I Love Sports"
2007	Emmy Award	Outstanding Original Music and Lyrics for *Saturday Night Live*; "Dick in a Box"
2007	MTV Movie Award Nomination	Breakthrough Performance for *Alpha Dog*
2007	Teen Choice Award Nomination	Choice Movie: Breakout Male for *Alpha Dog*

BIBLIOGRAPHY

BOOKS ABOUT JUSTIN TIMBERLAKE

Cefrey, Holly. *Justin Timberlake: Contemporary Musicians and Their Music*. New York: Rosen Publishing, 2009.

DeMedeiros, James. *Justin Timberlake: Remarkable People Series*. New York: Weigl Publishers, 2009.

Dougherty, Steve. *Justin Timberlake: Junk Food Tasty Celebrity Bios*. New York: Scholastic, 2009.

Dougherty, Terri. *Justin Timberlake: People in the News*. Farmington Hills, MI: Lucent Books, 2008.

Marcovitz, Hal. *Justin Timberlake: A View from the Paparazzi*. Broomall, PA: Mason Crest Publishers, 2008.

Napoli, Tony. *Justin Timberlake: Breakout Music Superstar*. Hot Celebrity Biographies. Berkley Heights, NJ: Enslow Publishers, 2010.

Roach, Martin. *Justin Timberlake: The Unofficial Book*. London: Virgin Books, 2003.

Smith, Sean. *Justin: The Unauthorized Biography*. New York: Pocket Books, 2004.

Tracey, Kathleen. *Justin Timberlake: Blue Banner Biography*. Hockessin, DE: Mitchell Lane Publishers, 2008.

ARTICLES ABOUT JUSTIN TIMBERLAKE

Bender, Michael. "It's Gonna Be You." *Seventeen*, July 2001, p. 99.

Collis, Clark. "Sexy Beat." *Entertainment Weekly*, February 9, 2007, pp. 32–37.

DePaulo, Lisa. "Locked and Loaded." *Gentlemen's Quarterly*, August 2006, pp. 110–17.

Friedman, Devin. "Icon." *Gentlemen's Quarterly*, September 2004, pp. 355–63, 428.

Hedegaard, Eric. "The Bachelor." *Rolling Stone Magazine*, January 23, 2003, p. 34.

Morgan, Laura. "Just 'NSide." *Seventeen*, November 2002, pp. 136–39.

Morgan, Laura. "'NSync Get Down & Dirty." *Seventeen*, July 2001, pp. 94–99.

O'Leary, Kevin. "Justin & Scarlett Fling or Real Thing?" *US Weekly*, January 29, 2007, pp. 70–71.

O'Leary, Kevin. "We're Done." *US Weekly*, October, 12, 2009, pp. 52–57.

Rapport, Adam. "The 10 Most Stylish Men in America." *Gentlemen's Quarterly*, March 2009, pp. 174–79.

Scaggs, Austin. "Justin Timberlake Revs Up His Sex Machine." *Rolling Stone Magazine*, September 21, 2006, pp. 50–56.

INTERNET

"ABC in Sync with Audience." *Studio Briefing Film News*, November 5, 2002. http://www.movieweb.com.

"ABC Sports' Singer-Reporter Timberlake May Be 'Sidelined.'" *Studio Briefing Film News*, December 24, 2003. http://www.movieweb.com.

AllMusic.com. http://www.allmusic.com.

Andreeva, Nellie. "Timberlake Developing Peruvian Comedy for NBC." Reuters, March 7, 2008. http://www.reuters.com.

Armstrong, Mark. "Timberlake to Fly Solo on MTV." *People*, August 20, 2002. http://www.people.com.

Associated Press, "Singer Justin Timberlake Closing New Memphis Golf Course for 6 Months for Renovation." *Metromix Nashville*, December 16, 2009. http://www.nashville.metromix.com.

Baker, K. C. "Ciara's Very Own Funny Guy: Justin Timberlake." *People*, May 14, 2009. http://www.people.com.

Balls, David. "Denters Album 'Has Timberlake Imprint.'" *Digital Spy News*, December 15, 2009. http://www.digitalspy.com.

"Banker Withdraws Jackson and Timberlake Lawsuit." *World Entertainment News Network*, February 11, 2004. http://www.wenn.com.

"Bass: 'I'm Gay and In Love.'" *ContactMusic.com*, July 27, 2006. http://www.contactmusic.com.

Belfuss, John. "Mirimichi Golf Course Is 'the Coolest Thing' Timberlake Has Ever Done." *The Commercial Appeal*, July 24, 2009. http://www.commercialappeal.com.

Berman, Liz. "Justin Timberlake Recalls His Grammy Surprise: No Rihanna!" *People*, March 27, 2009. http://www.people.com.

"Biel Was 'Stressed' Meeting Timberlake's Mother." *World Entertainment News Network*, November 5, 2008. http://www.wenn.com.

"Britney 'Cool' about Justin's Video." *World Entertainment News Network*, January 8, 2003. http://www.wenn.com.

"Britney, Justin, Lakers Sued." *TMZ Celeb*, November 13, 2009. http://www.tmzceleb.com.

"Britney's Pure Reputation May Be Soiled." *World Entertainment News Network*, September 27, 2001. http://www.wenn.com.

"Britney Spears: 'I've Only Slept with Justin.'" *World Entertainment News Network*, July 9, 2003. http://www.wenn.com.

"Cameron Diaz Sues *The National Enquirer*." *USA Today*, June 3, 2005. http://www.usatoday.com.

"CBS Defends Janet Jackson Telecast." *Studio Briefing Film News*, November 21, 2006. http://www.movieweb.com.

Chen, Joyce. "Gabourey Sidibe on Globe Nod: Justin Timberlake Said My Name!" *People*, December 15, 2009. http://www.people.com.

"Ciara Promises *Fantasy Ride* Follow-Up Will Be 'Pretty Hot.'" *MTV News*, December 9, 2009. http://www.mtvnews.com.

Dagostino, Mark. "Justin Timberlake to Appear on Jimmy Fallon's First Show." *People*, February 25, 2009. http://www.people.com.

Destino Restaurant, New York. http://www.destinony.com.

"Diaz Fights Back." *World Entertainment News Network*, December 27, 2004. http://www.wenn.com.

Diaz, Vanessa. "Justin Timberlake's Movie Date: His Mom." *People*, January 4, 2007. http://www.people.com.

"Diaz Wins Cheating Libel Case." *World Entertainment News Network*, July 31, 2005. http://www.wenn.com.

Ditzian, Eric. "Justin Timberlake on Michael Jackson: '99.97 Percent of His Songs Are Perfect.'" *MTV News*, October 20, 2009. http://www.mtv.com.

"Djs Fired After Starting Spears-Timberlake Hoax." *Hollywood.com*, June 20, 2001. http://www.hollywood.com.

Dyball, Rennie. "Christina Ricci 'So Impressed' by Justin Timberlake." *People*, March 3, 2007. http://www.people.com.

Elson, Rachel F. "Timberlake Stumbles with Broken Foot." *People*, November 20, 2002. http://www.people.com.

"The Elton John Story." *Studio Briefing Film News*, October 13, 2003. http://www.movieweb.com.

Entertainment Tonight Online. http://www.etonline.com.

"Fashion's Night Out Brings Out Crowds." Reuters, September 11, 2009. http://www.reuters.com.

Fields, Jackie. "Madonna and Justin Timberlake 'Tie One On' After Concert." *People*, May 1, 2008. http://www.people.com.

Goldsmith, Belinda. "Beyonce Tops People Fashion List." Reuters, September 12, 2007. http://www.reuters.com.

Grace, Melissa. "Justin Timberlake's Southern Hospitality Restaurant Slapped with Sexual Discrimination Lawsuit." *New York Daily News*, May 15, 2009. http://www.nydailynews.com.

Graff, Gary. "International Lineup Expected for Concert in Beijing." Reuters, December 18, 2009. http://www.reuters.com.

Graff, Gary. "Kings of Leon Readies Remix Album, Live DVD." Reuters, August 27, 2009. http://www.retuers.com.

Gray, Mark. "Inside Justin Timberlake & Pals $1M Fundraiser." *People*, October 22, 2008. http://www.people.com.

Gray, Mark. "Justin Timberlake Buys Drinks for Entire Vegas Club." *People*, September 2, 2009. http://www.people.com.

Gray, Mark. "Justin Timberlake's Mom Beats Him at Golf." *People*, October 16, 2009. http://www.people.com.

Gray, Mark. "TLC to Play First US Concert in 7 Years." *People*, August 25, 2009. http://www.people.com.

Grossberg, Josh. "Defunct 'NSync Still Bigger Than Your Favorite Band." *E! Online*, December 11, 2009. http://www.eonline.com

Grossberg, Josh. "'NSync Puppet Case Popped." *E! Online*, April 15, 2002. http://www.eonline.com.

Haralson, Jessica Gold. "Justin Timberlake Talks about His Game." *People*, September 29, 2008. http://www.people.com.

Harris, Chris. "Justin Timberlake Will Learn His Lesson in 'Shrek 3.'" *MTV News*, May 2, 2005. http://www.mtv.com.

Hiatt, Brian. "Kings of Pop." *Entertainment Weekly*, October 19, 2001. http://www.ew.com.

Internet Movie Database. http://www.imdb.com.

"Jackson Admits Super Bowl Stunt Was Intentional." *World Entertainment News Network*, February 4, 2004. http://www.wenn.com.

"Janet Convinced Justin to Perform at Super Bowl." *ContactMusic.com*, February 5, 2004. http://www.contactmusic.com.

"Johansson: 'I'm Not Dating Timberlake.'" *World Entertainment News Network*, February 13, 2007. http://www.wenn.com.

"Judge Rules against Super Bowl Viewer." Associated Press, May 27, 2005. http://www.ap.com.

"Justin's Hole-in-One." *People*, July 9, 2009. http://www.people.com.

"Justin Timberlake Gets Restraining Order against Karen J. McNeil." *Huffington Post*, October 23, 2009. http://www.huffingtonpost.com.

"Justin Timberlake: The Next John Madden?" *MTV News*, May 7, 2003. http://www.mtvnews.com.

"Justin Timberlake Inspires Art Gallery Exhibit." *People*, March 28, 2008. http://www.people.com.

"Justin Timberlake in Sync with Kid's Charity." *People*, September 28, 2009. http://www.people.com.

"Justin Timberlake: I Support Lance." *People*, July 27, 2006. http://www.people.com.

"Justin Timberlake Makes History as First *SNL* Host to Win Emmy." *Los Angeles Times*, September 13, 2009. http://www.latimes.com.

"Justin Timberlake's New Costar: The Eiffel Tower." *Jaunted: The Pop Culture Travel Guide*, November 3, 2009. http://www.jaunted.com.

"Justin Timberlake Sued by Restaurant Employee." *X17 Online News*, November 17, 2008. http://www.x17onlinenews.com.

"Justin Timberlake: Taylor Hicks 'Can't Carry a Tune in a Bucket.'" Associated Press, August 17, 2006. http://www.abclocal.go.com.

"Justin Timberlake Tells Leno He's Not Engaged—Or Pregnant." *People*, June 11, 2008. http://www.people.com.

Kaufman, Gil. "Justin Timberlake, Bruce Springsteen to Induct This Year's Rock Hall of Fame." *MTV News*, February 24, 2005. http://www.mtvnews.com.

Kilkelly, Daniel. "'Wardrobe Malfunction' Enters Dictionary." *Digital Spy*, August 14, 2008. http://www.digitalspy.com.

Klueber, Jillian. "Justin's Solo Act." *Time for Kids*, November 11, 2002. http://www.tineforkids.com.

Leach, Robin. "Justin Timberlake Hosts 'Last Chance for Change' Rally." *Las Vegas Sun*, October 11, 2008. http://www.lasvegassun.com.

Lehner, Marla. "Justin Says He Was 'Infatuated' with Britney." *People*, July 19, 2006. http://www.people.com.

"Leo's 'Five Friends'!" *The Insider News,* October 29, 2008. http://www.theinsider.com.

"Leona 'Was Nervous Meeting Timberlake.'" *Digital Spy,* November 12, 2009. http://www.digitalspy.com.

"*The Love Guru* Tops Worst Movie of 2008 List." December 3, 2008. http://www.icelebz.com.

"Madonna Invites Timberlake Back to the Studio." *World Entertainment News Network,* May 8, 2007. http://www.wenn.com.

Malkin, Marc. "Justin Timberlake: Stinkin' Up America, Too!" *E! Online,* July 10, 2009. http://www.eonline.com.

Martin, Laura. "Biel: 'I Listen to Justin's Music.'" *Digital Spy,* December 30, 2008. http://www.digitalspy.com.

"Matt Damon Wins 'Sexiest Man' Title." Reuters, November 15, 2007. http://www.reuters.com.

Mock, Janet. "Justin Timberlake Donates $200,000 to His Hometown." *People,* March 24, 2008. http://www.people.com.

"Molson Canadian Rocks for Toronto." http//Fact-Archive.com.

Moss, Cory. "Justin Timberlake Fan Killed in Alleged Hit-and-Run Outside Radio Station." *MTV News,* September 10, 2002. http://www.mtv.com.

MTV News Staff, "Madonna Sings 'Happy Birthday' to Justin Timberlake; Plus Rhianna, Beck, Warped Tour, George Clooney & More, in *For the Record.*" *MTV News,* January 31, 2008. http://www.mtvnews.com.

"*MTV Staying Alive* Picks Up *The Diary of Kelly Rowland.*" *AceShowBiz,* November 29, 2008. http://www.aceshowbiz.com.

Nichols, Michelle. "The Police Win Billboard Top Tour." Reuters, November 15, 2007. http://www.reuters.com.

Nichols, Michelle. "Timberlake Helping Duran Duran Get Sexy Back." Reuters, November 3, 2007. http://www.reuters.com.

"Nipplegate." *Studio Briefing Film News,* February 3, 2004. http://www.movieweb.com.

Orloff, Brian. "Justin Timberlake Explains Courtside PDA with Jessica Biel." *People,* April 23, 2009. http://www.people.com.

Park, Michael. "Peyton Manning Whips Justin Timberlake at Chinese." *People,* September 21, 2009. http://www.people.com.

Patel, Joseph. "'NSync Members Accused of Being Racists in Suit by Former Tour Manager." *MYV News,* December 17, 2003. http://www.mtvnews.com.

"Peas, Kings of Leon Top iTunes Best Sellers of 2009." Reuters, December 9, 2009. http://www.reuters.com.

Pedersen, Erik. "More 'Jizz' from *SNL's* Andy Samberg, Lonely Island." *Ace-ShowBiz*, December 15, 2008. http://www.aceshowbiz.com.

Perry, Beth. "Justin Timberlake Does 'Great Job' at the ESPYs." *People*, July, 17, 2008. http://www.people.com.

Peterson, Todd. "Justin Timberlake: A Motown No-Show." *People*, February 25, 2004. http://www.people.com

Popstar.com. http://www.popstar.com.

"*Precious* Star Reveals 'NSync Obsession." *World Entertainment News Network*, November 15, 2009. http://www.wenn.com.

Rappaport, Adam. "Justin Timberlake." *Gentlemen's Quarterly*, March 2009. http://www.gq.com.

Rashbaum, Alyssa. "Justin Timberlake Joins Stones at Toronto Benefit, Gets Pelted with Garbage." *MTV News*, July 31, 2003. http://www.mtv.com.

Rechtshaffen, Michael. "*The Open Road* Marred by Potholes." Reuters, August 31, 2009. http://www.reuters.com.

Reese, Lori. "How Does He Manage?" *Entertainment Weekly*, July 14, 2000. http://www.ew.com.

Reid, Shaheem. "Justin Timberlake Jumps on T-Pain's 'Can't Believe It' Remix." *MTV News*, November 10, 2008. http://www.mtvnews.com.

Reynolds, Simon. "Biel 'Takes Up Golf for Timberlake.'" *Digital Spy*, December 29, 2008. http://www.digitalspy.com.

Rice, Lynette. "Justin Timberlake, Tina Fey Take Gold at Creative Arts Emmys." *Entertainment Weekly*, September 13, 2009. http://www.ew.com.

Sarno, David. "Timberlake Signs On to Co-Star in Facebook Movie, *The Social Network*." *Los Angeles Times*, September 23, 2009. http://www.latimes.com.

"See Who Tops Barbara Walter's Fascinating List." *People*, December 7, 2007. http://www.people.com.

Seymour, Craig. "Show 'N Tell." *Entertainment Weekly*, August 4, 2000. http://www.ew.com.

Shriners Hospital for Children. http://www.shrinershq.com.

Silverman, Stephen. "Justin: Taylor Hicks 'Can't Carry a Tune in a Bucket.'" *People*, August 17, 2006. http://www.people.com.

Silverman, Stephen, with Laura Schreffler. "Justin Nabs Black Origin Music Prize." *People*, September 26, 2003. http://www.people.com.

Silverman, Stephen M. "Justin on Cameron: 'We're Not Engaged.'" *People*, September 4, 2006. http://www.people.com.

Silverman, Stephen M. "Justin Timberlake Opens Up about His Love Life." *People*, September 19, 2007. http://www.people.com.

Silverman, Stephen M. "Justin Timberlake Signs YouTube Singer to His Label." *People*, June 5, 2007. http://www.people.com.

Silverman, Stephen M. "Justin Timberlake: The Hoax 'Sucks.'" *People*, June 22, 2001. http://www.people.com.

Silverman, Stephen M. "Justin to Do Good, Lance to Do Movie." *People*, September 25, 2002. http://www.people.com.

Silverman, Stephen M. "Not Guilty Plea in 'NSync Fan Death." *People*, September 27, 2002. http://www.people.com.

Silverman, Stephen M. "Timberlake Burps His Way to Kids' Prize." *People*, April 14, 2003. http://www.people.com.

Silverman, Stephen M. "Timberlake Fan's Death: Murder Charge." *People*, September 12, 2002. http://www.people.com.

Sinclair, Tom. "Grand Ole Opry Teen Pop-ry." *Entertainment Weekly*, September 3, 1999. http://www.ew.com.

Slonim, Jeffrey. "Justin Timberlake Sinks Roots in New York." *People*, November 14, 2008. http://www.people.com.

"Snippet of Justin Timberlake's New Song 'Steppin' Out Tonight.'" *AceShowbiz*, October, 12, 2008. http://www.aceshowbiz.com.

"*SNL* Leaves Gift Box on YouTube." *Studio Briefing Film News*, December 22, 2006. http://www.movieweb.com.

Southern Hospitality Restaurant, New York. http://www.southernhospitality bbq.com.

Sperling, Nicole. "Anna Faris, Dan Aykroyd, Justin Timberlake Line Up for 'Yogi Bear.'" *Entertainment Weekly*, November 5, 2009. http://www.ew.com.

Stack, Tim. "Justin Timberlake Exclusive: The Singer on His New Album (or Lack Thereof) and Current iPod Favorites." *Entertainment Weekly*, March 25, 2009. http://www.ew.com.

Stack, Tim. "Timbaland on Miley Cyrus: She's the Next Justin Timberlake." *Entertainment Weekly*, November 12, 2009. http://www.ew.com.

"Stars Join Forces to Ban Guns." *World Entertainment News Network*, December 4, 2000. http://www.wenn.com.

Stransky, Tanner. "Adam Samberg Dishes on Justin Timberlake and Their Latest 'SNL' Short, 'Motherlover.'" *Entertainment Weekly*, May 11, 2009. http://www.ew.com.

Stransky, Tanner. "10 Biggest Celebrity Scandals of the Decade." *Entertainment Weekly*, December 23, 2009. http://www.ew.com.

Stroup, Kate. "Jessica Biel Considers Justin Her Private Present." *People*, December 9, 2008. http://www.people.com.

Susman, Gary. "'Inside' Out." *E! Online*, October 30, 2001. http://www.eon line.com.

Takahashi, Corey. "Burning Question." *Entertainment Weekly*, March 24, 2000. http://www.ew.com.

Tauber, Michelle. "Justin Timberlake." *People*, June 24, 2005. http://www.people.com.

Tewksbury, Drew. "Justin Timberlake's Patriotic Shout-Out." *People*, July 5, 2007. http://www.people.com.

"Timberlake Accepts Libel Damages." *BBC News*, August 24, 2005. http://news.bbc.co.uk.

"Timberlake and Aguilera Tour Faces Ticket Troubles." *World Entertainment News Network*, June 17, 2003. http://www.wenn.com.

"Timberlake + Biel Rally for Obama." *World Entertainment News Network*, October 13, 2008. http://www.wenn.com.

"Timberlake Christens Eco-Friendly Golf Course." Associated Press, July 26, 2008. http://www.ap.com.

"Timberlake Donates $100,000 to Irwin Zoo." *Brisbane Times*, October 30, 2007. http://www.brisbanetimes.com.au.

"Timberlake Goes Public with Biel." *World Entertainment News Network*, May 17, 2007. http://www.wenn.com.

"Timberlake Hits Out at Celebrity Culture." *San Francisco Chronicle*, April 4, 2007. http://www.sfgate.com.

"Timberlake in Racist Slur Accusation." *ContactMusic.com*, December 15, 2003. http://www.contactmusic.com.

"Timberlake Kicks Off Espy Awards with a Laugh." *World Entertainment News Network*, July 17, 2008. http://www.wenn.com.

"Timberlake: 'Let's Wait for Britney's Baby Pictures.'" *San Francisco Chronicle*, October 25, 2005. http://www.sfgate.com.

"Timberlake Refused to Take Acting Classes." *World Entertainment News Network*, December 28, 2006. http://www.wenn.com.

"Timberlake Regrets Grammy Awards Talent Showcase." *World Entertainment News Network*, March 22, 2007. http://www.wenn.com.

"Timberlake Sings 'I Apologize'—Jackson Doesn't." *Studio Briefing Film News*, February 9, 2009. http://www.movieweb.com.

"Timberlake Slimes Up a Storm at Kids Choice Awards." *World Entertainment News Network*, April 2, 2007. http://www.wenn.com.

"T.I. to Shoot 'Dead and Gone' Music Video with Justin Timberlake." *AceShowBiz*, December 11, 2008. http://www.aceshowbiz.com.

Tourtellotte, Bob. "David Beckham Tops Rivals on a 'Man's Man' List." Reuters, October 25, 2007. http://www.reuters.com

Travers, Eileen. "Fans Sing to Justin on His 26th Birthday." *People*, February 1, 2007. http://www.people.com.

Tucker, Ken. "Reba McEntire in Fine Company on 'Duets.'" Reuters, September 15, 2007. http://www.reuters.com.

Vena, Jocelyn. "Adele Apologizes for Snubbing Justin Timberlake at Grammys." *MTV News*, March 5, 2009. http://www.mtvnews.com.

Vena, Jocelyn. "Ciara Heats Up with Justin Timberlake in 'Love Sex Magic.'" *MTV News*, March 23, 2009. http://www.mtv.com.

Vena, Jocelyn. "Justin Timberlake, Kanye West Make GQ's 10 Most Stylish Men List." *MTV News*, February 17, 2009. http://www.mtv.com.

Vena, Jocelyn. "Justin Timberlake on Michael Jackson: He 'Was the Baddest'!" *MTV News*, June 30, 3009. http://www.mtvnews.com.

Vena, Jocelyn. "Justin Timberlake Retires 'SexyBack,' Rocks with 50 Cent at Las Vegas Concert." *MTV News*, October 20, 2008. http://www.mtvnews.com.

Vena, Jocelyn. "Justin Timberlake's William Rast Makes Fashion Week Debut." *MTV News*, February 18, 2009. http://www.mtvnews.com.

Vena, Jocelyn. "Justin Timberlake Wants You to Answer 'The Phone.'" *MTV News*, April 15, 2009. http://www.mtv.com.

Vena, Jocelyn. "Miley Cyrus, Justin Timberlake More Ring in the New Year with MTV: A Look Back." *MTV News*, December 30, 2009. http://www.mtvnews.com.

Vena, Jocelyn. "Rihanna Tell GQ 'Nobody' Helped Her Deal with Chris Brown Assault." *MTV News*, December 15, 2009. http://www.mtvnews.com.

Vena, Jocelyn, with Saimon Kos. "Usher and Justin Timberlake Battled It Out for Justin Bieber. *MTV News*, September 12, 2009. http://www.mtvnews.com.

Verner, Richard. "Woodland Hills Connects with Facebook Movie." *Los Angeles Times*, November 9, 2009. http://www.latimes.com.

"Viacom to Pay Record $3.5 Million to Settle FCC Indecency Cases." *Online NewsHour*, November 24, 2004. http://www.pbs.org/newshour/updates.

"Video: Alicia Keys Helps Honor Her 'Unstoppable' Global Family." *People*, December 3, 2009. http://www.people.com.

Vineyard, Jennifer. "Timberlake Pulls Out of Motown Special in Wake of Protests." *MTV News*, February 25, 2004. http://www.mtv.com.

Vineyard, Jennifer. "Why Is Justin Timberlake's *Alpha Dog* Flick So Controversial?" *MTV News*, January 4, 2007. http://www.mtv.com.

Wang, Julia. "Letterman Puts Justin Timberlake on the Hot Seat." *People*, September 12, 2006. http://www.people.com.

"West Pays Tribute to Timberlake Inspiration." *World Entertainment News Network*, August 22, 2007. http://www.wenn.com.

"William Rast Launches Retail Expansion with First Three Stores." *Timberlake-Justin.com*, November 3, 2009. http://www.timberlake-justin. com.

Wolk, Josh. "Boys Trouble." *Entertainment Weekly*, October 6, 1999. http:// www.ew.com

Wolk, Josh. "'N Rage." *Entertainment Weekly*, November 4, 1999. http://www. ew.com.

"Worried TV Bosses Add Tape Delays to Grammys." *ContactMusic.com*, February 4, 2004. http://www.contactmusic.com.

"You Love Her: Britney Spears Named the Biggest Star of the Decade." *Reel Loop News*, December 31, 2009. http://www.reelloopnews.com.

"Zellweger Fronts New Cancer Campaign." *World Entertainment News Network*, December 15, 2009. http://www.wenn.com.

INDEX

About the Author

KIMBERLY DILLON SUMMERS is a freelance writer and editor and full-time mother residing in Rockford, Illinois. She graduated from Iowa State University with a degree in journalism and mass communication. She is a former editor of NTC/Contemporary Publishing, where she worked on the popular *Chase's Calendar of Events*. She has written *Miley Cyrus: A Biography*, published in 2009, for Greenwood Press's Biography Series. She has written biographical information for the Internet site Allmusic.com. Her articles have also been published by the Bridges Initiatives Inc., and she creates newsletters and writes financial articles for Rock Valley Federal Credit Union located in Loves Park, Illinois.